SUPER HAWKS
The Seattle Seahawks' 2013 Championship Season

TONY OVERMAN/Staff photographer

THE NEWS TRIBUNE
[thenewstribune.com]

The Olympian
www.theolympian.com

Linebacker
Malcolm Smith,
who was named the
MVP of Super Bowl
XLVIII, celebrates
after his 69-yard
interception return
in the second
quarter.
— *JOE
BARRENTINE/
Staff photographer*

This book is available in quantity at special discounts for your group or organization.
For further information, contact:

Triumph Books LLC
814 North Franklin Street
Chicago, Illinois 60610
Phone: (312) 337-0747
www.triumphbooks.com

Printed in U.S.A.
ISBN: 978-1-60078-897-0

The News Tribune* and *The Olympian
David Zeeck, Publisher
Karen Peterson, Editor
Dale Phelps, Managing Editor
David Montesino, Visuals Editor
Darrin Beene, Sports Editor
Eric D. Williams, Beat Writer
Todd Dybas, Beat Writer
Dave Boling, Columnist
John McGrath, Columnist
Kenny Via, Staff Writer
Joe Barrentine, Photo Editor
Lui Kit Wong, Photographer
Tony Overman, Photographer
Scott Stoddard, Photographer
Randy McCarthy, Copy Editor

Content packaged by Mojo Media, Inc.
Joe Funk: Editor
Jason Hinman: Creative Director

A special thanks to Emily and Richard Weinberg, valued members of the 12th Man contingent.

Front and back cover photos by TONY OVERMAN/Staff photographer

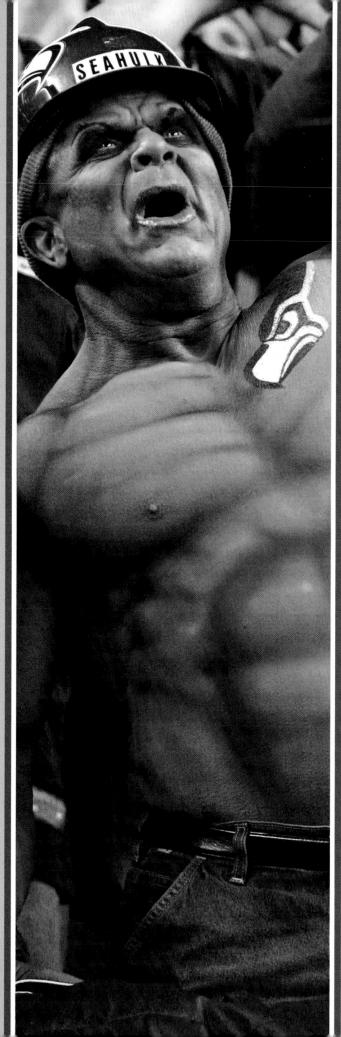

Contents

INTRODUCTION

By Kenny Via

For 38 years, it was always something. There was always some reason why the Seattle Seahawks were not the NFL's best.

But finally, on Feb. 2, 2014, they were.

Seattle erased years of frustration with an emphatic 43-8 victory over the Denver Broncos in Super Bowl XLVIII at MetLife Stadium in East Rutherford, N.J.

The Seahawks' first Super Bowl win was fueled by self-confidence and years of unwavering belief.

Denver brought the NFL's No. 1 offense — a squad that scored 606 points in the regular season.

Seattle countered with the league's top defense.

Hype for the showdown went into overdrive after Seattle's NFC championship win when Seahawks cornerback Richard Sherman shouted his greatness into TV cameras.

The focus shifted to Broncos quarterback Peyton Manning vs. Seattle's Legion of Boom secondary, labeled by many the best in the NFL.

But when the teams faced off, the tailor-made matchup never lived up to the billing. The Seahawks' suffocating defense did what it had since coach Pete Carroll took charge — dominated.

Denver started the game on offense and snapped the ball over Manning's head for a safety. The Broncos next possession was a three and out.

Seattle piled on for a 15-0 lead in the second quarter. Late in the half, with Denver threatening to finally score, linebacker Malcom Smith intercepted Manning and ran 69 yards for a touchdown.

The score was 22-0, and the Seahawks never looked back.

Carroll's vision had come true.

The coach, who won seven Pac-10 titles and two national championships at USC, brought his "win forever" philosophy to the Northwest before the 2010 season and challenged his players to "always compete."

The Seahawks obliged.

"These guys started a long time ago; it took four years to get to this point," Carroll said while clutching the Vince Lombardi Trophy after his team's victory. "They've never taken a step sideways or backwards from going forward to make this team the way it is now."

At the beginning of the season, quarterback Russell Wilson posed a question to his teammates: "Why not us?"

The architects of the 2013 Seahawks — owner Paul Allen, coach Pete Carroll and general manager John Schneider — celebrate after bringing the first Super Bowl title to Seattle.
— *JOE BARRENTINE/Staff photographer*

Seattle spent the 2013 season showing over and again why it was the most dominant team in the NFL.

With 13 regular season wins, a bruising rubber-match victory over the rival San Francisco 49ers in the NFC championship and the Super Bowl win, Seattle earned the championship they'd set out to capture.

They likely changed a few minds along the way.

Wilson led Wisconsin to the Rose Bowl, but his pro potential was questioned because of his 5-foot-10-inch frame. Carroll and general manager John Schneider ignored all that and drafted Wilson in the third round in 2012.

The quarterback returned the favor with back-to-back Pro Bowl seasons.

It's a common theme throughout Seattle's roster — players whose talent was questioned before they found success with the Seahawks.

All-Pro Sherman was a fifth-round draft pick out of Stanford. Even his college coach, Jim Harbaugh, passed on him in the draft as the head man for the 49ers.

Sherman landed in Seattle, led the NFL with 20 interceptions over his first three seasons and made a critical pass deflection against San Francisco to clinch Seattle's Super Bowl berth.

Wide receiver Doug Baldwin went undrafted before earning a job with the Seahawks in 2011. Pundits called him and the rest of Seattle's receivers "pedestrian" before Baldwin torched the 49ers for 106 yards and went on to score a touchdown against the Broncos in the Super Bowl.

Strong safety Kam Chancellor and cornerback Byron Maxwell were fifth-round draft picks. Both made big plays in the win over Denver.

Linebacker Smith was drafted in the seventh round. He was named the Super Bowl MVP.

Seahawks quarterback Russell Wilson, a second-year starter, reaches for coach Pete Carroll. Wilson had doused Carroll with Gatorade following the Seahawks' Super Bowl XLVIII victory.
— *TONY OVERMAN/Staff photographer*

Running back Marshawn Lynch was considered damaged goods when Seattle traded two mid-round draft picks for him in 2010. Lynch was soon dubbed "Beast Mode" for his bruising running style.

Even Carroll — fired from head coaching jobs with the New York Jets and New England Patriots — had his doubters.

Many wondered whether the coach's upbeat attitude could inspire professionals to victory.

Carroll and Schneider met the challenge with shrewd enthusiasm.

They turned over Seattle's roster at a dizzying rate. They drafted left tackle Russell Okung and safety Earl Thomas with their first two picks. They brought in castoff veterans and undrafted free agents.

They found speed — lots of it — and players who fit their scheme.

After back-to-back 7-9 seasons, the band of misfits came together in 2012. They produced an 11-5 record and the franchise's first road playoff victory since 1983 before suffering heartbreaking defeat in Atlanta.

The Seahawks returned with a chip on their shoulders.

In 2013, they ran through opponents with dominating precision, punching their ticket to the showdown with Manning and the Broncos.

Led by Sherman, Thomas and Chancellor, the Seahawks defense did its part. Wilson and Lynch powered the offense, and Seattle took its first championship crown.

It was the culmination of a movement that started four years earlier, and the manifestation of Wilson's question: Why not them?

Seattle answered in dramatic fashion, and silenced those who had questioned the Seahawks' coach and players.

It was a special season — one that can truly be described as super. ∎

Super Bowl XLVIII took place in East Rutherford, New Jersey, but Seattle's 12th Man made its presence known. — *TONY OVERMAN/Staff photographer*

SUPER BOWL XLVIII
Game Date: February 2, 2014
Location: East Rutherford, New Jersey
Score: Seahawks 43, Broncos 8

HAWKS BY A MILE

Top-ranked defense throttles Denver's mighty offense

By Todd Dybas

The Seattle Seahawks won America's biggest sports event by never giving Denver a chance.

Not a sniff. Not a drive that brought fear or a hint of a challenge from the Broncos. Seattle's brash, top-ranked defense showed a superiority even they wouldn't have predicted.

The Broncos were throttled, bottled by a simple, efficient and fierce Seattle defense.

The Seahawks tore up a Denver offense that had scored the most points in league history. At the end, blue and green confetti shot into the air. Coach Pete Carroll was drenched with Gatorade. A season-long journey while under scrutiny to be the best ended with the Seahawks as just that.

Seahawks 43, Broncos 8. The Seattle Seahawks are Super Bowl XLVIII champions, delivering the downtrodden sports region its first professional men's title in 35 years and the organization its first since its inception in 1976 in its second Super Bowl appearance.

"It's been a long year," Carroll said. "But the team was really dedicated to getting this done and now we can say we're world champions."

Icon Peyton Manning finished with a misleading Super Bowl-record 34 completions. He joked last week he had not asked brother Eli — who threw five interceptions in the same stadium against Seattle in mid-December — for advice about the Seahawks. Eli won't be asking him now, the Seahawks likely a taboo subject in that household now. A befuddled Manning finished with two interceptions and a fumble.

Seattle was able to pressure Manning with just four rushers. Menacing strong safety Kam Chancellor walloped Demaryius Thomas early and had an interception. Cliff Avril, a master of the strip-sack, clipped a piece of Manning's arm when he was throwing. Super Bowl MVP Malcolm Smith intercepted the resulting duck throw and returned it 69 yards for a touchdown.

Denver wasn't permitted any easy inch while the game was still competitive, which it wasn't for long. The Seahawks scored 12 seconds into each half. They picked up a safety on the first play from scrimmage when Manning's famous audibling backfired. When he stepped to the line to make an

Quarterback Russell Wilson targets wide receiver Jermaine Kearse for a 23-yard touchdown in the third quarter of the Seahawks' 43-8 victory over the Broncos in Super Bowl XLVIII.
— *TONY OVERMAN/Staff photographer*

Defensive end Chris Clemons and defensive tackle Clinton McDonald force Broncos running back Knowshon Moreno to fumble late in the first quarter. Broncos guard Zane Beadles recovered the ball. — *TONY OVERMAN/Staff photographer*

adjustment, the ball was snapped. It flew into the end zone. He said it was a cadence issue.

In hindsight, the Seahawks' 2-0 lead appears it would have been sufficient. That's how smothering the defense was.

The discussion is open now. Seattle's season-long assault of offenses was finished off by forcing the Broncos to succumb. The 2013-14 Seahawks have elbowed their way into conversations that will include the 2000 Baltimore Ravens, 1985 Chicago Bears, Pittsburgh Steelers teams of the 1970s, or any other defensive juggernaut professed to be the best.

"I told you we're the best defense ever," defensive lineman Michael Bennett said. "We could have played anyone today and did the same thing."

Led by a top-down approach with the league's best secondary, the Seahawks allowed teams to throw shallow. That was Denver's approach all season. It's an ill-advised style against a fast-closing, hard-hitting Seahawks defense.

Denver stuck with it regardless. After Chancellor delivered his shot, the tone was set.

"They started dropping like flies," linebacker Bobby Wagner said.

At media day during Super Bowl week, the NFL set up five high-profile positions. The coach and quarterback were naturals for two. The other three spots were occupied by members of the Seahawks' vaunted secondary: Chancellor, free safety Earl Thomas and cornerback Richard Sherman, a rarity to have such fame in the secondary.

Blessed with salary cap flexibility by the emergence of stars such as Russell Wilson and Sherman still on rookie contracts, the Seahawks were able to bolster the defensive line in the offseason.

In came Bennett and Avril from free agency. They boosted a stifling and rotating defensive line. Pushing into Manning's space all game during

Super Bowl MVP Malcolm Smith returns his interception of a Peyton Manning pass for 69 yards and a touchdown in the second quarter.
— *TONY OVERMAN/Staff photographer*

Percy Harvin
helped the
Seahawks continue
their dominance
at the start of the
second half with
an 87-yard kickoff
return for
a touchdown.
— *TONY
OVERMAN/Staff
photographer*

an unseasonably warm February evening in the Northeast, the Seahawks' defense left no doubt if the cliché "defense wins championships" was still viable.

The Seahawks' 36 consecutive points to start the game were a Super Bowl record. It was the first time Manning had trailed in a game by 29-plus points since 2002. It was the first game in which Manning's club was held to fewer than 17 points since he joined Denver in 2012.

The blue-and-green celebratory confetti was blown off the field within a couple hours of the game's conclusion. That was a fleeting celebration.

Not the title. For the rest of their lives, each Seahawk will have a hand-worn gleaming reminder of Super Bowl XLVIII. When they look at those rings, they'll remember one of the best defenses in NFL history.

That can be a debate. What's unequivocal is that the Seahawks are world champions. ■

Opposite: Wide receiver Doug Baldwin dives for a 10-yard touchdown early in the fourth quarter. It was the last Seahawks score on the night.
Above: The 12th Man showed up in full force at MetLife Stadium, as Seahawks fans kept the noise level up all night to disrupt Denver and helped cheer Seattle to a victory.
— *JOE BARRENTINE/Staff photographer*

MALCOLM SMITH NAMED SUPER BOWL MVP

Linebacker part of dominating performance

By John McGrath

Malcolm Smith didn't mind the notoriety that eluded him after his end-zone interception in the NFC Championship Game assured the Seattle Seahawks of a trip to Super Bowl XLVIII.

Smith figured — in the words of the late Frank Sinatra, the New Jersey native associated with a more famous song that blared over the sound system of MetLife Stadium — the best is yet to come.

"Hopefully," Smith told me during a pre-Super Bowl media session that found him all but ignored, "we'll get another that trumps it in this game. I'll focus on that. I'd rather have a Super Bowl ring than the greatest interception in the NFC Championship Game."

Along with his teammates, Smith earned a ring on Feb. 2, thanks to the Seahawks' 43-8 obliteration of the Denver Broncos. But the former seventh-round draft choice from USC also was given the keys to a 2014 Chevrolet Silverado as Super Bowl XLVIII's Most Valuable Player.

Two weeks after his interception in the NFC Championship Game was overshadowed by events that immediately preceded and followed it, Smith picked off a Peyton Manning pass in Seahawks territory and never looked back during a 69-yard return for a touchdown. Smith also participated in 10 tackles, broke up a pass and recovered a fumble.

"Man, it's incredible," Smith said. "It's the way our defense is set up. We just run to the ball.... I'm just the one today. It happens all the time like this."

Reflective of Seattle's domination of the No. 1 single-season offense in NFL history is the fact strong MVP cases could have been for several Seahawks on both sides of the ball.

Kam Chancellor's interception of a first-quarter pass — it floated into his hands — was among the difference-making plays the strong safety contributed on a night that included five unassisted tackles and two passes defensed.

Defensive end Cliff Avril, who at 6 feet 3 and 260 pounds should've been overmatched by the Broncos' 6-7, 320-pound Orlando Franklin, put a bull-rush on the tackle and arrived in time to impede Manning's delivery on the throw Smith intercepted.

Wide receiver Percy Harvin touched the ball only twice during the regular season while recovering from hip surgery. After he spent most of the NFC divisional playoff against New Orleans on the sideline with a concussion, it was reasonable to presume anything he contributed during the ultimate playoff game would be a bonus.

Linebacker Malcolm Smith, who played for Pete Carroll at USC, hoists the Vince Lombardi Trophy after Seattle's 43-8 victory over Denver in Super Bowl XLVIII. — *TONY OVERMAN/Staff photographer*

But on a night that the Broncos' record-setting offense appeared overmatched and, ultimately, overwhelmed by a Seahawks defense that turned Super Bowl XLVIII into the equivalent of a first-round knockout, Harvin also made a compelling case as an MVP.

After a bad snap resulted in a Broncos safety to open the game, Harvin's 30-yard gain on an end around came on the Seahawks' second snap, and put the Seahawks in position to kick the field goal that gave them the distinction of earning the first 5-0 lead in Super Bowl history.

Harvin added 15 yards on a similar play near the end of the first quarter, then he put the game out of reach by fielding the second-half kickoff.

A Denver comeback wouldn't have been unfathomable. Baltimore owned a 28-6 third-quarter advantage last year in the Super Bowl, and ended up having to hold on to win 34-31 against San Francisco in a thriller. But Harvin's 87-yard return served as emphatic proof that only one team — the team in the white jerseys — would be in position to return home with the Vince Lombardi Trophy.

"Those guys had so much belief in me," said Harvin. "Even when I wasn't practicing, those guys were saying, 'You're going to score on this,' and I'm like, 'I'm not even on the field practicing yet.'"

Quarterbacks are typically the most obvious MVP selections, and Russell Wilson's performance — 18-for-25 passing for 206 yards and two touchdowns — was worthy of consideration, if for no other reason than his spectacular passing rating of 123.1. (For perspective on that number, Manning set a Super Bowl record of 34 completions — and finished with a 73.5 rating.)

But by the time the passing game with Wilson achieved a second-half rhythm that kept the Broncos on their heels, the blowout was on the brink of historic.

In 47 previous Super Bowls, no team had been shut out, and yet the Seahawks had a 36-0 lead until the final play of the third quarter, when Manning finally managed a touchdown pass that did little to alleviate the humiliation.

"Watching the film coming into the week," Seahawks linebacker Bobby Wagner said, "we'd seen that they hadn't played a defense like ours. They hadn't played a defense that flies around like we do, that hits like we do, and we just do it every single play.

"We're a part of history. A hundred years from now, y'all are going to remember this team."

Wagner's prediction might be a bit optimistic, as I'm not sure many of us will be in shape, 100 years from now, to talk about the night the Hawks conquered four decades of franchise frustration.

But I understand the spirit of his words: the Seahawks put on a show so balanced, so inspired and so comprehensively impressive that it was difficult to determine who deserved an individual award.

Smith was given the title to the vehicle, but the title of Super Bowl MVP could have gone to any of several teammates.

It's something the president might keep in mind when the world champion Seattle Seahawks visit the White House. ∎

Super Bowl MVP Malcolm Smith, a seventh-round draft pick in 2011, celebrates his pick-six just before halftime. — *JOE BARRENTINE/Staff photographer*

24
RUNNING BACK
MARSHAWN LYNCH

Actions matter, words don't

By Eric D. Williams • September 5, 2013

In the hills near his waterfront home in Richmond, Calif., near Oakland, most mornings during the offseason you can find Marshawn Lynch climbing makeshift stairs he had built for his daily training regimen.

"It's just putting in the time," he said. "That's it. It ain't nothing too special to it, just putting in the time and the effort."

Reports of Lynch not showing up for part of the Seattle Seahawks' offseason program made news back in Washington. However, Lynch diligently trained at home, reporting to training camp in the best shape of his life.

"He's really worked," Seahawks running backs coach Sherman Smith said. "And we've just talked about him getting better this year, so in the fourth quarter when we go into our four-minute offense, he stays on the field. I told him that's your job — to win the game for us in the end.

"So when we have to run the ball 10 times, 12 times — whatever it is — that he's not on the sideline eating Skittles and drinking water."

While other Seahawks generate more headlines — think Richard Sherman — and national attention — Russell Wilson — it is Lynch who is the engine that makes Seattle's run-first attack go.

Lynch set a career high for rushing yards (1,590) and attempts (315) in 2012. His 2,531 rushing yards between Week 9 of the 2011 season and the end of 2012 is the most over that time frame.

He rushed for 100 yards or more in 16 of his previous 25 games heading into 2013. He was voted to the Pro Bowl the past two seasons and has earned the nickname Beast Mode because of his physical, relentless running style.

But you won't hear him talk about it, because Lynch evades reporters like the would-be tacklers he dodges and plows through on the field.

"I just feel it's crazy how much time people put into this media stuff," he said. "If they put as much time into the media as they put into something else in life, they'd be great at doing something.

"I mean, what am I going to talk about?"

Marshawn Lynch acknowledges Seahawks fans following a touchdown run against the Rams in the regular season finale. — *TONY OVERMAN/Staff photographer*

It's not the spotlight Lynch avoids as much as it is who he is.

"He was always a real quiet kid," Lynch's mother, DeLisa Lynch said. "But if he set his mind toward it, then that's what was going to happen. He's been like that."

The Birth of Beast Mode

DeLisa Lynch didn't want her son playing varsity football at Oakland Tech. She watched him excel as a running back in youth football. But the boys were much bigger and rougher tackling her son during his freshman year.

"It was different than Pop Warner," she said. "They were crunching and hitting, and I was like, 'No, my baby ain't playing no varsity. That's out.' But for some reason over the summer, he just grew. He just got real big and real strong."

By the time he was a sophomore, Lynch was starting at running back. According to Larkins, Lynch was more a scat back then, known more for making people miss than running over them.

But the transformation from a Barry Sanders-type runner to what NFL observers see now on Sundays took years of work in the weight room, along with daily work out on the field with Larkins, cousin Josh Johnson, who now serves as the backup quarterback for the Cincinnati Bengals, and Larkins' son, Virdell Larkins Jr., now a defensive backs coach at New Mexico Highlands University.

"Once he came and started running with power, that was Beast Mode," he said. "I was his strength coach. They would lift weights every day, until 9 o'clock at night. Six days a week we trained. The seventh day was Sunday, and they watched film. So it was non-stop."

When Lynch returns home, part of his workout includes bag drills with Larkins back at his old high school field, which he considers getting back to the basics of what established his power and balance as a runner.

The drill is simple — a runner has to maintain his balance while keeping his knees high running over bags on the ground while trainers on either side of him try to knock him off balance or strip the ball out.

"Being able to get back to those bag drills, that's just automatic — that's consistency," Lynch said. "That's something I've been doing, and I'll continue to. I think I'll keep doing the bags even when I'm done.

"Those are defenders. I know they're just bags, but to a running back it teaches them to never stop their feet from moving and keep their legs high."

Larkins also kept it simple on game days — one defender should never tackle you.

"We started counting the YAC yards — yards after contact," Larkins said. "And when we would come in and watch film, I'd ask him, 'So one person can tackle you?'"

He said that if Lynch got tackled by just one person, he'd have up-downs to do the following practice on Monday.

"He was a kid that was always going to persevere regardless, and I think that's how he runs," he said. "He lives for today, knowing that tomorrow is coming. But he has to make what's happening right now."

No story about Lynch would be complete without mentioning his affection for Skittles.

His mother first introduced him to the candy during youth football games. But the story is a little different than how it's been recycled on TV. "I would always have candy in my purse — just something to kind of calm him down," DeLisa Lynch said. "So I would give him the Skittles before the game, and tell him, 'Here baby, you eat these. These are you power pellets.' ... It was just a joke for me and him."

Get Some Square in You

Ask Lynch about personal goals for the 2013 season and you likely won't get a peep. But a number he does care about is the 21 kids under the age of 18 that have been shot and killed in Oakland since 2011.

In order to fight that statistic, Lynch started his annual football camp every summer at Oakland Tech. The free camp, now in its seventh year, has grown to 600 participants, and offers kids a chance to interact with Lynch and other pro athletes up-close.

Also, Lynch lets kids know that there's more to life outside the streets of Oakland.

"We had to bury a few kids that had been there that a lot of the kids had seen," Lynch said. "So it was more of how we perceive the community being from Oakland. Making it out of Oakland and going to other places, seeing other places. And being able to come back to Oakland and share that with the youth is something that helps open their eyes."

Lynch has had success stories emerge from the camps. DiAndre Campbell and Marcus Peters play football at the University of Washington. DeJon Gomes plays safety for the Detroit Lions. But there's also kids that have moved on to attend college, become coaches and are active in the business world.

"He has been a great mentor for me," Peters said. "I give him a call when (there is) stuff I need (answers for). I talk to him, and he keeps in touch with all of us from the Oakland area, you know. He is just there if we need anything, just to call and talk to."

Lynch was one of those kids from Oakland headed down the wrong path. He showed a lack of interest in school, skipping classes, something DeLisa Lynch worked hard to change.

"I would work like noon to 8, and Marshawn would have like English and Spanish in the morning," she said. "And he was having trouble in those classes. And I would go with him and sit in class. I did that for my son."

While attending her son's classes, she recognized that Marshawn had trouble seeing the chalkboard up front and took him to have his eyes checked. She found out that Beast Mode needed glasses.

"Once he got glasses, he was able to see better, and it helped him," she said.

Lynch stayed local for college, attending Cal where he became the fourth player in school history to gain over 3,000 yards rushing. The Buffalo Bills then selected him with the 12th overall pick in the 2007 draft but his time with the team was marred by off the field incidents, which is how the Seahawks came to acquire him four games into the 2010 season.

In 2008, Lynch had his license revoked after he hit a 27-year-old woman and kept driving. The next year, he was suspended for three games after pleading guilty to a misdemeanor gun charge.

Lynch also has an alleged DUI charge still winding its way through the Alameda County district court system.

The Seahawks understood the risks in giving up fourth-round and fifth-round picks to secure the services of Lynch. But they felt comfortable enough with Lynch to offer him a four-year, $32 million deal in free agency during the 2012 offseason.

Other than the pending DUI case, Lynch has stayed out of trouble.

"The growth he's experienced in his maturity level is huge," said Kevin Parker, a family friend who recruited Lynch to Cal. "He's had his stumbles and setbacks, but he's continued to move forward."

'A Unique Personality'

You never know what Marshawn is going to do next.

He can be walking and joking with fellow teammates one minute, and all of sudden break out in a full sprint through the locker room.

Sometimes you will spot him riding his mountain bike along the road in front of the team's facility from his home nearby in Renton.

Before practice starts, he'll work with the defensive linemen on pass rush drills, with his gloves attached to his face mask.

"He has a very unique personality," Johnson said. "He's hyper — a big, grown kid."

"They see the dreads and the gold (teeth) and think, "Oh, he's a thug.'" Larkins said. "But they don't know his heart."

Former Seattle running back Justin Forsett, now with Jacksonville, was Lynch's roommate at Cal. A son of a preacher, the humble Forsett is much different than the spontaneous Lynch. Still, the two are good friends, with Forsett returning to Oakland each summer to help out with Lynch's camp.

"We have two different personalities, but it's one of those things where real recognized real," Forsett said. "He has a genuine heart, and I have a genuine heart. And we just stayed close friends."

Smith calls Lynch the most talented running back he's ever coached, and that includes his days in Tennessee working with Eddie George.

"He can do all of it," Smith said. "He can make you miss with power. He has decent speed. He doesn't have speed that some other guys have. And he has elusiveness. Now, if you're a tackler, you don't know what you're going to get from him. Is he going to stick his foot in the ground and run by me? Or is he going to try and run over me?"

Forsett takes it even a step further, saying Lynch will go down as one of the best runners to ever play the game.

"He just has a unique balance of speed and power," Forsett said. "A lot of guys just have power, or they just have speed. But he has it all. He can shake guys, or he can run through you. And I think that's what keeps the defensive players off guard.

"There's countless runs that I've seen in school, and I was there in Seattle for Beast Quake. So I've seen a lot of it first hand. He's one of those guys that will go down I believe as one of the best to ever do it. He's got that type of skill set. He runs with such toughness and violence. Right now, Marshawn and Adrian Peterson are at the top of the game."

Seahawks offensive line coach Tom Cable called Lynch football brilliant, saying what made him so special is his ability to quickly adapt to new schemes or changes in the offense.

"He doesn't need a lot of reps," Cable said. "He doesn't need to go to the board and rehash it over and over, or look at it on film. He can get it right then and there. So that's a real gem in terms of skill set.

"He wants to be special, and I think that's our mentality. We try to do everything better than someone else can do it, or has done it. And he's adaptive to that. Plus, I think he understands he's profiting from that, too."

Offensive lineman Breno Giacomini says Lynch's relentless running style rubs off on the rest of the offense.

"It's pretty cool to block for him really," Giacomini said. "It's awesome. He's the type of runner every offensive lineman wants. So we're very lucky to have him, and I'm very lucky to block for him.

"We just respect the hell out of him. We respect the way he runs, and that's why we're trying to be perfect out there, so he can be perfect."

But for Lynch, the accolades and praise don't matter — wins do.

"I just go out there and play like it's my last game," he said. "Everybody's living through social media. Everybody is like a surrogate. Nobody's real anymore. If you don't have a thousand followers on Instagram, you're not smacking. Nobody wants to talk to you.

"That's not real life. Don't feed into that. What's real is this life." ■

Marshawn Lynch celebrates after scoring one of his three touchdowns in Seattle's 29-3 rout of the 49ers in September. — *LUI KIT WONG/Staff photographer*

REGULAR SEASON

Game Date: September 8, 2013
Location: Charlotte, North Carolina
Score: Seahawks 12, Panthers 7

VICTORY IN ADVERSITY

Seattle puts away Carolina with strong effort in fourth quarter

By Eric D. Williams

They've learned from their mistakes.

The Seattle Seahawks turned the agonizing pain of losing to Atlanta in the NFC divisional playoffs the previous season into a positive.

They want to make sure that it doesn't happen again.

Paying attention to the small things during training camp paid off in the form of a grind-it-out, 12-7 victory over the Carolina Panthers at Bank of America Stadium in the season opener for both teams.

"We needed as a team to see some adversity," Seahawks cornerback Richard Sherman said. "I talked about it last night in the meeting; we were going to see some adversity. Last year, we didn't really see too much adversity until the playoffs.... I think us getting this kind of game early is going to help propel us throughout the season."

The victory was Seattle's first in a road opener since defeating Detroit, 9-6, in 2006. The Seahawks are 4-6 in road openers since 2000.

"It was hard today, really hard," Seattle coach Pete Carroll said. "The thing I liked about it is our guys hung tough. We made the plays when we needed to make them. We finished the game with the ball in our hands, which we always like. And we get out of our first game on the road with a win."

Seattle played ragged at times, which was expected for the first game of the season. The Seahawks finished with nine penalties for 109 yards and also failed to score a touchdown from inside Carolina's 20-yard line on three occasions.

Still, when the Seahawks needed a play to turn the game, they made it.

After grabbing a 3-0 lead on Steven Hauschka's 27-yard field goal midway through the second quarter, the Seahawks saw the Panthers respond with a scoring drive of their own on the following possession, marching 80 yards on 11 plays with Cam Newton hitting Steve Smith for a 3-yard touchdown pass.

Carolina's stout defense made that lead stand until the fourth quarter. Seattle got another Hauschka field goal, this one from 40 yards, cutting the margin to 7-6 with just over two minutes remaining in the third quarter. But the Seahawks finally grabbed the lead for good in the final quarter.

Russell Wilson passed for a season-high 320 yards in the season opener against the Panthers. — *AP Images*

After Russell Wilson failed to connect with Stephen Williams on a deep pass down the right sideline, the Seattle quarterback went back to a similar route to Jermaine Kearse on the next play. And Wilson connected with the University of Washington and Lakes High School product for a 43-yard touchdown with 10 minutes, 21 seconds to play.

"I just kind of read that play," Wilson said. "I went through my progressions really, to be honest with you, and he was my second read. And he just did a great job of attacking the football."

Wilson finished with 320 yards passing on 25-for-33 accuracy, including the touchdown pass to Kearse.

It was Wilson's second 300-yard performance in the pros and second in as many games. The other was a 385-yard, two-touchdown performance against Atlanta in the playoffs the previous season.

Up 12-7, all Seattle's defense had to do was get a stop. The Seahawks failed in similar situations in the 2012 season against Arizona, Detroit, Miami and in the NFC divisional playoff game at Atlanta — all come-from-behind wins for the opposing team.

Sunday would be different.

Carolina put together a promising drive, quickly marching into Seattle territory. And the Panthers were on the verge of getting into the end zone when running back DeAngelo Williams burst through the middle of Seattle's defense on a run, turning up the right sideline.

However, safety Earl Thomas chased him down and punched the ball out, with defensive tackle Tony McDaniel emerging from the pile with the loose ball 8 yards from Seattle's goal line, ending Carolina's chances for a potential go-ahead score with 5:43 to play. Williams also lost a fumble last year against the Seahawks that led to Seattle's winning score when he was stripped by Brandon Browner, who also recovered the fumble.

"It's a huge play," Carroll said. "And nobody takes more pride than Earl knocking that ball loose. It is where we live and die with taking care of the football. They got it off of us once today in a crucial situation.

"We were fortunate to get that one when we needed it most. They really had a lot of momentum going at that time. And it was just a gigantic play in this football game."

From there, the Seahawks salted away the game with a 12-play drive to run out the clock.

"You always want to open your season with a win," Seattle tight end Zach Miller said. "But even more so because we've got a big game next week. Obviously, there will be a lot of headlines that go along with it. But we're excited and looking forward to it." ∎

Opposite: Marshawn Lynch finished the 2013 regular season with the sixth-most rushing yards among running backs (1,257), the second-highest total in his eight season-career. **Above:** Jermaine Kearse and Russell Wilson celebrate after connecting on a 43-yard touchdown pass. — *AP Images*

REGULAR SEASON

Game Date: September 15, 2013
Location: Seattle, Washington
Score: Seahawks 29, 49ers 3

HAWKS WIN ONE-SIDED SHOWDOWN

Seattle's defense makes some noise with three picks

By Eric D. Williams

Two games into the 2013 season, there's no question who rules the NFC West.

It's the Seattle Seahawks.

"There were a lot of pundits and ignorant idiots that picked us to lose this game," Seahawks cornerback Richard Sherman said. "Please don't doubt us again."

In a highly anticipated, heavyweight match-up with last year's NFC representative in the Super Bowl, the Seahawks beat the 49ers at their own game.

They bullied them.

Seattle ground out 172 rushing yards in a 29-3 humbling in front of a CenturyLink Field-record crowd of 68,338 onlookers Sunday evening.

The Seahawks have now outscored San Francisco 71-16 in the past two meetings, both wins in Seattle.

While the running game rumbled, Seattle's defense led the way, holding the 49ers explosive offense to 207 total yards.

A week after he threw for 412 yards and three touchdowns in a win over Green Bay, Niners quarterback Colin Kaepernick was held to a career-low 107 yards passing as a starter.

"We did everything we needed to do tonight on defense," Seahawks coach Pete Carroll said.

Kaepernick threw only three interceptions in 218 regular-season attempts last season. The Seahawks picked him off three times on Sunday, with Kam Chancellor, Earl Thomas and Sherman each getting an interception.

With the win, the Seahawks now sit alone atop the NFC West division, jumping out to a 2-0 record to start a season for the first time since 2006. The Seahawks have won 10 of their 11 home openers since 2003.

The victory also gave Pete Carroll a fitting birthday present on his 62nd birthday.

The game was unexpectedly suspended because of unsafe weather conditions with lightning visible from the stadium at 6:05 p.m., with the two teams scoreless and 3:13 remaining in the first quarter.

The Seahawks needed the break. Up until that point, Seattle had managed just 27 yards of total offense. The Seahawks were 0-for-3 on third downs, and quarterback Russell Wilson was 0-for-6 passing with an interception to Eric Reid.

Carroll said his team made some much-needed

Linebacker Bobby Wagner blocks for Richard Sherman as the cornerback returns an interception during the Seahawks' 29-3 victory over the 49ers. — *LUI KIT WONG/Staff photographer*

37

adjustments during the weather delay.

"It was a great opportunity for us," Carroll said. "I'm sure they were doing the same thing. We did all kinds of things in all phases, wherever it was needed. We coached throughout the time, other then when the music was blaring in the locker room."

San Francisco grabbed momentum early when Craig Dahl blocked Seattle punter Jon Ryan's punt. Seahawks linebacker Malcolm Smith recovered the ball on the Seattle 33-yard line. However, the Seahawks' defense held firm. On third-and-goal from the 5-yard line, cornerback Walter Thurmond tipped a pass intended for San Francisco tight end Vernon Davis at the goal line, and safety Earl Thomas corralled the rebound, returning the ball to Seattle's 12.

The Seahawks took an early lead when Smith was held by San Francisco fullback Bruce Miller while chasing after Kaepernick in the Niners' end zone, resulting in a safety and a 2-0 lead.

Seattle then upped its lead to 5-0 on a Steven Hauschka 30-yard field goal with 5:52 remaining in the half.

In the second half, the Seahawks took control of the contest on a 10-play, 80-yard drive, capped by a Marshawn Lynch 14-yard touchdown run, giving Seattle a 12-0 lead with 9:12 remaining in the third quarter.

The 49ers responded with a nine-play, 71-yard drive, culminating in a Phil Dawson 21-yard field goal.

But Seattle scored 17 consecutive points to close out the game, including two Lynch touchdowns consisting of a 7-yard pass and a 2-yard run and a Hauschka 37-yard field goal. Lynch finished with 98 yards on 28 carries.

"We did what we expected to (tonight)," Sherman said. "I think you guys (pointing to reporters) expected something different. You guys expected something a little more Kaepernicking — a couple of these (kisses his bicep).

"We didn't expect any of that. We expected guys to play disciplined ball." ◼

The divisional showdown between the Seahawks and the 49ers included a 60-minute weather delay, but the rain in Seattle didn't faze Russell Wilson.
— *LUI KIT WONG/Staff photographer*

Safety Kam Chancellor celebrates with teammates after picking off 49ers quarterback Colin Kaepernick. It was the Seahawks' third interception of the game. — *LUI KIT WONG/Staff photographer*

REGULAR SEASON

Game Date: September 22, 2013
Location: Seattle, Washington
Score: Seahawks 45, Jaguars 17

HAWKS DOMINATE ON PAPER, ON FIELD

Seattle had too much talent in easy victory

By Todd Dybas

Taped up paper covered the slim, vertical window in the door to the visiting coaches' booth, which opens into the press box.

The translucent glass is only about four inches wide and half a yard long. Despite Jacksonville's coach being an important former Seahawks employee and Seattle being ample favorites, the Jaguars chose a manual cover-up in an attempt to assure the sanctity of club secrets.

Although Jacksonville coach Gus Bradley had insider knowledge of the Seahawks' organization — he was previously Seattle's defensive coordinator — that insight and a temporary paper window shade weren't enough because of the wide gap in talent between the Jaguars and Seahawks.

So, the Seahawks took the Jaguars on their expected woodshed visit, beating Bradley's bunch, 45-17, on Sunday at CenturyLink Field.

The Seahawks have allowed the fewest points in the league and scored the second-most. "We've got a long ways to go, though," quarterback Russell Wilson said.

This is the point where Wilson launches into Pete Carroll-speak. Each week is a championship week. Build a day at a time, a

practice at a time, a week at the time. Salivate when thinking of repetition.

It was the focus of the week when facing Bradley, who was in charge of the Seahawks' defense from 2009-12. He applied the nickname of "Deuce" to Earl Thomas. His relationship with the players and Carroll was one with depth.

Bradley believes in it so much, he has taken much of it to Jacksonville. The Seahawks knew he knew what they knew.

That's why the Seahawks' quarterbacks took the field believing what they were seeing as opposed to carrying presumptions.

"What you see is what you get," backup quarterback Tarvaris Jackson said. "Don't go out here and just because they do this, think you're going to get that. What you see, that's how you play it."

The fact that Jackson had almost a quarter-and-a-half full of on-field views explains the tenor of the game.

The Seahawks were ahead 31-0 with 11 minutes, 41 seconds remaining in the third quarter after Wilson's fourth touchdown pass of the day.

Russell Wilson threw a season-high four touchdown passes in the Seahawks' decisive 45-17 victory over the Jaguars. — *TONY OVERMAN/Staff photographer*

Wilson was on the field for just two more series after that, for once turning a Sunday into a day of leisure for him.

"I think, offensively, we're starting to come into our own now, we're starting to get into a rhythm," Wilson said. "We have to continue that."

That possibility was made simpler by a lack of penalties. The Seahawks had nine penalties in the opener and 10 more last week during the drubbing of the San Francisco 49ers.

They committed just four penalties against the Jaguars, half by the offense.

Following the first series, a rare three-and-out, it was clear the Jaguars would not be stopping the Seahawks, who also finally did not stop themselves.

Wilson threw his first two touchdowns to tight end Zach Miller. Miller came into the game with three touchdowns in two seasons with Seattle. He was so wide open on the first it appeared Jacksonville had thought him a leper.

Sidney Rice caught two himself. Steven Hauschka kicked a 21-yard field goal. Jackson later hit Doug Baldwin for a diving 35-yard score Carroll said "might be the catch of the year for us so far."

Across the field from a friend, Carroll took the rare approach of throttling back in the third quarter. Jackson and rookie running back Christine Michael were sent in, as were several defensive substitutes.

The game's outcome was so clear a week after the ferocity and din of opposing the 49ers, even voluble cornerback Richard Sherman had little to say. Though, he had a warning.

"It's early," Sherman said. "Anything can happen. [In 2012] Arizona was 4-0 ... early on. It's always what you are doing in November and December that really counts." ◾

Wide receiver Golden Tate, who was Russell Wilson's favorite target in the Seahawks' win over the Jaguars, tries to slip past Jacksonville cornerback Demetrius McCray.
— *TONY OVERMAN/Staff photographer*

HEAD COACH

PETE CARROLL

Coach's philosophy centers around getting, keeping football

By Dave Boling • September 24, 2013

Pete Carroll claims it was the first thing he said to the Seattle Seahawks when he took the job.

Not hello, pleased to meet you, or I'm jacked/amped/pumped to be here.

But, "it's about the ball."

And, as it turns out, he's been right. Getting the ball and keeping it. Maintaining custody when it's yours, and absconding with the ball when the other guys have it.

The three top teams in the NFL's turnover ratio rankings through the first three weeks of the 2013 season (Kansas City plus-9, Seattle plus-6 and Chicago plus-6) all started 3-0.

"We have preached it from the first thing I ever said to these guys from the first day I walked in here," Carroll said. "And they hear it every week and it's a constant emphasis that hopefully makes the point that you've got to be great at taking care of (the ball) and you've got to go after, if you want to determine wins, (because) it usually works out that way."

From Carroll's arrival in 2010 through Week 3 of 2013, the Seahawks were 20-3 in games when they had the advantage in the turnover ratio.

Three games into the 2013 season, they had forced 10 turnovers (five interceptions and five fumbles) while committing four (two interceptions and two lost fumbles).

They forced 31 turnovers in 16 games in 2012 and were at nearly a third of that total through just three games. Factoring in their own turnovers, their plus-13 mark last year was good enough to be fifth in the NFL.

Against San Francisco in Week 2, they pilfered three passes from quarterback Colin Kaepernick, who threw just three picks in 2012.

Seattle took two more from Jacksonville quarterback Chad Henne in Week 3, including an impressive diving grab by linebacker Bobby Wagner and a probable point-saving pick in the fourth quarter by safety Kam Chancellor, who returned it 32 yards.

Not only are they getting the ball more often, they're more efficient at returning interceptions, too, averaging 20 yards per return this season to 14 yards in 2012.

When the ball is in the air, or bouncing loose on the ground, the Seahawks' defense is trained to attack. It's the theme of Thursday practices, when sessions stress getting to tipped balls and knocking it loose from ballcarriers. Even

The Seahawks have enjoyed immense success since coach Pete Carroll's arrival in 2010, with three playoff wins, an NFC Championship title and now the franchise's first Super Bowl win in its second appearance. — *LUI KIT WONG/Staff photographer*

linemen spend time diving on fumbles and recovering the ball.

"It's how we want to play," Carroll said. "Taking care of the football and getting after it. To us, it's the biggest factor that determines winning and losing."

Cornerback Richard Sherman last week put it in more colorful terms. "It's like throwing meat out to wolves sometimes ... everybody wants the ball."

Carroll said it reflects the personality of the team.

The Seahawks won by a 45-17 score, but the defense was upset that Jacksonville finished with so many points.

"I don't feel the happiest right now," Chancellor said after the Jacksonville game. "That's too many yards (214 passing by the Jaguars).

"We were upset they had like, what ... 200 passing yards?" safety Earl Thomas asked. "I don't think that's us."

Carroll liked that his defenders were dissatisfied with their performance.

"It's good, their standards are set very high," he said. "We love the attitude of our guys. We've been together long enough now they know what they want to get done and how they're going to get it done. That shows you where their heads are ... they want to do great stuff."

Offensively, meanwhile, quarterback Russell Wilson threw his second interception of the season and lost a fumble when he was sacked.

"We're trying to throw no-hitters every time we go out in terms of turning the football over," Carroll said. "It's the deciding factor so often we're going to continue to champion that as our No. 1 emphasis." ■

Pete Carroll celebrates the Seahawks' victory in the regular season finale over the Rams, clinching the NFC West title and home-field advantage.
— *TONY OVERMAN/Staff photographer*

REGULAR SEASON

Game Date: September 29, 2013
Location: Houston, Texas
Score: Seahawks 23, Texans 20 (OT)

SEAHAWKS STAGE TEXAS-SIZED RALLY

Seattle scores game's final 20 points to stun Texans in Houston

By Todd Dybas

For most of the day, the heart of Texas was a dark and hellish place for the Seattle Seahawks.

Seattle trailed the Houston Texans by 17 points at halftime. An offensive line without three starters provided little resistance. The first half was abysmal for the Seahawks.

That's when the halftime discussion tilted to Atlanta and the rally there last season against the Falcons in the playoffs.

The Seahawks went home short that day after trailing by 20 points. They left Texas elated.

Richard Sherman's 58-yard interception return for a touchdown with 2 minutes, 40 seconds to play in the fourth quarter produced a stunning tie. Russell Wilson's legs and savvy put the Seahawks in a position to force overtime on a day where little worked for the offense.

Both helped Seattle trample road doubt and leave Reliant Stadium as 23-20 winners after a 45-yard overtime field goal by Steven Hauschka on Sunday.

The Seahawks advanced to 4-0 for the first time in franchise history after scoring 20 unanswered points to leave Houston with a win made of luck and grit.

Part of the narrative hanging around the Seahawks is a question about their road worthiness. A disjointed season-opening win at the Carolina Panthers did little to quell the wonder produced by a 3-5 regular-season record away from CenturyLink Field in 2012.

The 2012 season ended on the road when the rally against the Falcons was short in the divisional round of the playoffs.

Sunday, when nothing was working — the Texans had more sacks (two) than the Seahawks had passing yards (zero) late in the second quarter — there was a fix.

"When things are going great, it's easy," wide receiver Golden Tate said. "To look at these guys' eyes at halftime, when we were getting dominated on both sides, we still had the confidence that we could come back and make plays and get back into the game."

That comeback waited until the fourth quarter. Running back Marshawn Lynch (17 carries, 98 yards) talked with Wilson. He had a suggestion: "Hey, Russ. Just take over."

There was not another option.

Throughout the day, Wilson was crushed and

Richard Sherman's interception return for a touchdown late in the fourth quarter of the nailbiter against the Texans tied up the score and set the stage for Steven Hauschka's game-winning field goal in overtime.
— *AP Images*

chased by a Texans line blowing through the Seahawks' offensive line.

After sliding at the end of runs earlier in the game, Wilson began to scramble upfield with purpose. He finished the third quarter with three rushes for 3 yards. He ended the game with 10 carries for 77 yards.

"I just decided, I'm going to step up (in the pocket). I'm going to slide a little more," Wilson said. "If it's not there, I'm going to take off and see what happens."

Wilson was on the go in the Seahawks' second possession of overtime. He scrambled 7 yards for a first down. He hit Doug Baldwin for a 7-yard completion that turned into a 22-yard gain after Houston cornerback Kareem Jackson slammed Baldwin to the ground for a 15-yard unnecessary roughness penalty.

Two Lynch carries later, the Seahawks were in position for Hauschka's 45-yard winner.

"They handed it to us every way they wanted to in the first half," Seahawks coach Pete Carroll said. "But, once it got going, we could feel the defense's play and

Russell's (play) was off the chart."

Wilson had 43 rushing yards on the opening drive of the fourth quarter. He also hit Baldwin up the sideline for what was initially ruled an incompletion.

Carroll challenged and won. Instead of a fourth-and-7 play, the Seahawks had a 24-yard gain to convert just their second third down of the day.

Lynch pushed the Seahawks into the end zone when he took a pitch 3 yards untouched. He also sprinkled in typical runs that make his shoulder pads appear to be constructed from concrete. In a game for bulls and banging, Lynch was one of the few Seahawks up to the task throughout.

The Seahawks' defense caught up to him after the half. Houston kicked a 42-yard field goal with a second remaining in the second quarter. It wouldn't score again.

"There was a lot of undisciplined things that we can clean up," safety Kam Chancellor said. "Guys saw a big stadium, a good, physical team and everybody wanted to do more.

"Once we calmed that down, they didn't score any points."

As expected, Houston defensive end J.J. Watt, the reigning NFL defensive player of the year, could not be tamed. He had eight tackles, half a sack and three quarterback hurries.

He also provided a succinct summary of the outcome from Houston's point of view.

"Sucks," Watt said.

Just the opposite of what the undefeated Seahawks are thinking. ■

Opposite: Steven Hauschka, who made 33 of 35 field goals in the 2013 regular season, clinched the victory over the Texans with a 45-yard field goal in overtime. **Above:** Russell Wilson kept the Seahawks alive in their first overtime game of the season against the Texans and would do so again in overtime against the Buccaneers in Week 9. — *AP Images*

REGULAR SEASON
Game Date: October 6, 2013
Location: Indianapolis, Indiana
Score: Colts 34, Seahawks 28

SEAHAWKS' UNDEFEATED RIDE ENDS

Colts score 11 unanswered points to drop Seahawks to 4-1

By Todd Dybas

The end of games for the Seattle Seahawks is often the beginning of a glorious final step.

Tight, pressure-filled contests have been delectable outings for Seattle the past two years.

This season, while far outscoring opponents in the fourth quarter the Seahawks had dominated their first four foes.

Not Sunday.

The Indianapolis Colts beat the Seahawks, 34-28, after scoring 11 unanswered fourth-quarter points at Lucas Oil Stadium, snapping Seattle's nine-game regular-season winning streak.

A coverage bust and flags contributed to the loss. A blocked field goal was a major swing. A ruling after Jeron Johnson appeared to recover a blocked punt in the end zone left the Seahawks with two points instead of six.

Nothing was more detrimental than the Seahawks' frequent stalls around the Colts' 30-yard line. Seattle had six drives run out of air just before surfacing.

The Colts countered with conversions and odd-angled throws that became completions.

Indianapolis was 7-for-12 on third-down plays. Seattle was 2-for-12. The Seahawks are 4-1 as a result.

"We had our shots," Seattle coach Pete Carroll said. "We didn't get the ones we needed."

The trend started early.

Steven Hauschka, a busy man Sunday with five field-goal attempts, hit a 42-yarder on Seattle's opening drive. The Seahawks were stuck at the Colts' 24 when they couldn't convert a third-and-15, leaning on Hauschka for points.

Hauschka was summoned again on Seattle's fourth drive, which petered out at the Colts' 30. This kick was blocked, scooped up and returned 61 yards by Delano Howell for an Indianapolis touchdown.

The Seahawks drove to the Indianapolis 18-yard line, 23-yard line and 28-yard line in the third quarter. Each endeavor ended with Hauschka field goals.

Two of those three drives closed with incomplete third-down passes from Russell Wilson. He was erratic through the air — just 15-for-31 — but he scampered for 102 yards.

The final polish that usually comes from the Seahawks — a 44-7 edge in the fourth quarters of

Wide receiver Jermaine Kearse beats Colts cornerback Vontae Davis to the ball with a 28-yard touchdown reception.
— *AP Images*

After review, officials confirmed the call of a safety instead of a touchdown. Carroll was surprised.

"I was sure they were (going to overturn it)," Carroll said.

The Colts rocketed back into the game when a coverage bust between cornerback Richard Sherman and safety Earl Thomas ended with a 73-yard touchdown catch for T.Y. Hilton, who finished with a career-high 140 yards receiving. Howell's 61-yard return of Hauschka's blocked field goal vaulted the Colts ahead, 14-12.

The Seahawks countered with jabs from Hauschka, but their lead never again stretched to double figures. Hilton scored in the third quarter on a 29-yard TD pass from Andrew Luck, and third-string running back Donald Brown dived in from 3 yards out to put the Colts up 31-28 with 8:55 remaining in the game.

Seattle didn't cross the 50-yard line again. Adam Vinatieri kicked a 49-yard field goal to cap the scoring.

"The game was there to be had for us in a number of different ways," Carroll said.

Sherman was terse, a tad clichéd, but also unbowed afterward.

"We'll flush it right after we watch it tomorrow," Sherman said. "We're 4-1 and lead our division. C'mon. Same old."

Except Sunday, it wasn't. That's why the Seahawks are no longer undefeated. ∎

the first four games — did not show up against the Colts.

"We've got a find a way to get more touchdowns," Wilson said. "Once we do that, that game won't be close."

Based on the Seahawks' start, it appeared as if the game might not be close.

Seattle built a 12-0 first-quarter lead, finally finding life at the start of a game. The Seahawks had scored 10 first-quarter points over their first four games.

The lead would have been larger if officials had agreed with Carroll's assessment of a blocked punt. Former Lakes High School and University of Washington standout Jermaine Kearse blocked the Colts' punt attempt at the 27. Johnson sprinted toward the ball and fell on it in the end zone, sliding out of the back with the ball tucked against his body.

Opposite: Marshawn Lynch eludes Colts safety Antoine Bethea on his way to racking up 102 rushing yards on the day. **Above:** Russell Wilson connected with receivers Golden Tate and Jermaine Kearse for two touchdowns against the Colts. — *AP Images*

REGULAR SEASON
Game Date: October 13, 2013
Location: Seattle, Washington
Score: Seahawks 20, Titans 13

NOT PRETTY, BUT A 'W' FOR SEAHAWKS

Game doesn't go as planned, but Hawks shake off Titans

By Todd Dybas

Often, a direction preferred is not the direction traveled. The ride can be circuitous and bumpy.

In the Seahawks' discombobulated but nonetheless satisfying 20-13 win over the Tennessee Titans on Sunday at CenturyLink Field, Seattle took unanticipated routes.

Consider the largest gain of the day:

The Seahawks stood at their 20-yard line with first down in a 10-all tie with a team they were favored to beat by two touchdowns.

Quarterback Russell Wilson wheeled right, and the offensive line flowed with him — as did the Titans' defense.

Coming out of the huddle, Wilson warned running back Marshawn Lynch that even though everything was designed to go elsewhere, to be ready.

"Hey, you never know," Wilson said.

Lynch slipped out of the chaos to a silent patch of turf on the left. Wilson hit him for a 55-yard gain.

Undeterred by the mania that persisted much of the game, the Seahawks moved to 5-1. Coupled with New Orleans' late loss at New England, Seattle was back tied atop the NFC.

"It was a weird game," Seahawks center Max Unger said.

After kicker Steven Hauschka was bloodied when trying to make a tackle following a late second-quarter kickoff, the Seahawks were forced to use a backup crew to attempt a field goal just before halftime.

Safety Chris Maragos, who held for four years in college, was the new holder. Punter Jon Ryan, typically the holder, lined up for a 21-yard attempt. Maragos didn't handle the snap, then fumbled when desperation spurred him to run. Titans cornerback Jason McCourty picked up the fumble and zipped up the left sideline for a 77-yard touchdown.

On the previous play, the Seahawks had killed the clock with a spike. They had two seconds remaining and a decision to make. Looking at third-and-goal from the 4, coach Pete Carroll sent out the makeshift kicking unit.

Disaster followed.

"I screwed it up," Carroll said. "We should have just gone for it."

The Seahawks almost had another mess in the fourth quarter. Lynch was popped at the Tennessee 2-yard line. The ball went airborne, Titans

Marshawn Lynch tries to shake off Titans defensive lineman Mike Martin and safety Bernard Pollard.
— *TONY OVERMAN/Staff photographer*

linebacker Zach Brown eyed it, and the crowd braced. Brown tried to wrap his arms around the ball without success. It bounced off him, then the turf before it was fielded by former college shortstop Wilson.

"I saw the big hop, and went and got it," Wilson said.

The Seahawks picked up three points on the drive when Hauschka hit a 29-yard field goal, giving them a 13-10 lead. A Lynch touchdown with 7:33 remaining put them up, 20-10, on a day filled with errors. Some were costly, others weren't cashed in.

Lynch fumbled. Fullback Derrick Coleman fumbled. Wide receiver Sidney Rice fumbled. Maragos fumbled.

"The ball was greased today," Carroll said.

Snuffing out the oddities was the Seahawks' defense.

Bitter after last week's busts against the Indianapolis Colts, the defense did not allow a touchdown. Safety Earl Thomas made his third interception of the season, as did cornerback Richard Sherman.

The Seahawks controlled Titans running back Chris Johnson (12 carries for 33 yards), who has devolved from a rusher who gained 2,006 yards in 2009 to someone who was benched at one point Sunday.

Seattle trailed, 3-0, after Tennessee's Rob Bironas hit a 38-yard field goal with 5:16 to go in the first quarter. Lynch's 1-yard touchdown run put the Seahawks in front before the Titans retook the lead on McCourty's stunning return.

Hauschka hit from 31 and 29 yards in the second half after passing concussion tests at halftime. His only miss this year was a blocked kick against the Colts.

Though the past two weeks haven't followed the expected route, the Seahawks are tied for the conference lead midway through October.

"There's 32 teams in the league," defensive end Red Bryant said. "I'm pretty sure a lot of them would like to be in the position we're in." ∎

Richard Sherman's fourth-quarter interception helped set up a Marshawn Lynch touchdown on the subsequent drive that gave the Seahawks a two-score lead over the Titans.
— *TONY OVERMAN/Staff photographer*

3

QUARTERBACK

RUSSELL WILSON

Doubts about Wilson? They're ancient history

By John McGrath • October 16, 2013

When the Seattle Seahawks visited Arizona during Week 7, it marked just more than a year — 13 months and eight days, to be precise — since they previously faced the Cardinals at University of Phoenix Stadium.

In the chronological context of a 4.54 billion-year-old planet, 13 months and eight days is a microsecond. If time were quantified as money, it would be the equivalent of 50 cents in Paul Allen's pocket.

But for an NFL playoff contender that has evolved as quickly as the Seahawks, the subplots surrounding their 20-16 defeat in the 2012 season opener are the stuff of a fossil-bone dig.

It wasn't surprising the Hawks lost a game they had several chances to win. What's surprising, in retrospect, is that their inability to score a last-minute touchdown despite taking seven snaps inside the Cardinals' 20-yard line — including four snaps from the 6 — surprised nobody.

This was a team supposedly built to finish somewhere between 7-9 and 9-7. The bar wasn't set high. Seattle would take advantage of the seismic-event acoustics at home and struggle to score enough points to eke out the typical 17-14 decision on the road.

A major reason for the offense's absence of firepower was its unproven quarterback. Fans had seen glimpses of Russell Wilson's play-making potential during the exhibition season, but once the stakes were intensified in real games, against authentic starters, Wilson likely would regress to the mean of a rookie given more responsibility than a rookie can handle.

Coach Pete Carroll already had made the controversial decision to start Wilson instead of Matt Flynn, the veteran backup acquired to replace Matt Hasselbeck. One bold gamble was enough for Carroll, who wasn't inclined to roll the dice again and require Wilson to win games. Better that he not commit the turnovers that lose them.

Of the Seahawks' first 12 plays on second down against the Cardinals, they ran nine times. When Wilson got clearance to go to the air, he usually delivered a low-risk, low-reward throw

Russell Wilson has led the Seahawks to the playoffs in each of his first two seasons as a starter, putting debates about his height and ability to rest. — *JOE BARRENTINE/Staff photographer*

that counted as a pass on the stat sheet but served as a lateral.

Wilson ended up with 34 attempts, but his 18 completions netted only 153 yards and one touchdown. The Cardinals pressured him early and often — he took three sacks — and while the rookie remained composed and put the Hawks in position to win, the consensus opinion of Wilson's performance was that it merely had been adequate.

Matt Flynn to the rescue? That was the hot-button issue of the sports talk shows during the week preceding the 2012 Hawks' home opener against the Cowboys. Wilson had the heart and brains of an NFL quarterback, no doubt, but standing on the south side of 5-feet-11, he didn't have the height.

Recalling the 120-degree room temperature of the Wilson vs. Flynn debate is worth some giggles today. It's like paging through a high school yearbook full of photos of students wearing earnest smiles and really stupid clothes.

Reasonably informed football fans argued the merits of a rookie quarterback who would go on to star in the Pro Bowl against the merits of a journeyman quarterback?

Really? This was a debate topic?

Aside from Wilson's startling ascent from game-managing rookie to face-of-the franchise quarterback, the Seahawks pretty much brought the same group to Arizona that they did in 2012. Leon Washington was no longer returning kicks and punts, and fullback Michael Robinson was gone, along with outside linebacker Leroy Hill and wide receiver Braylon Edwards. Among the coaches, Dan Quinn had replaced defensive coordinator Gus Bradley, who accepted the mission-almost-impossible gig of reviving the

Jaguars in Jacksonville.

Otherwise, the 2013 Seahawks were the 2012 Seahawks, only with dramatically enhanced expectations. Losing to Arizona in 2012 fit into the norm of a so-so team that had no legitimate Super Bowl aspirations. If the Seahawks lost to Arizona in 2013, Seattle area telephone crisis lines would have been jammed.

"A really indicative game of the league," Carroll said after the Cardinals survived the Hawks' comeback drive. "The margin is just so short."

Unless it isn't. In the December 2012 rematch against Arizona, the Seahawks won, 58-0.

The morphing of the 2012 Hawks from a mediocrity whose mission was to keep the game close into late-season steamrollers didn't happen overnight. Wilson, with the resolve of Thomas Edison at a science fair, had to work to gain Carroll's trust as a quarterback capable of the miraculous, rather than a quarterback whose sole role was to minimize mistakes.

But the trust has been established.

Thirteen months and eight days after Wilson's debut opened to mixed reviews, the Seahawks returned to the scene of his NFL baptism. The Hawks were expected to win, and win without counting on Wilson to oversee the last-minute comeback that fell short in 2012.

Then again, this is football and you never know, especially after a freak week that turns the practice cycle into chaos.

Wilson is familiar with the drill. He craves it. He owns it.

As for the 2012 opener at Arizona, this is a memory best kept in an air-tight bag made to contain a foul stench. The memory reeks of yesterday, and all Russell Wilson can think about is tomorrow. ■

As comfortable running the ball as he is throwing it, Russell Wilson rushed for 539 yards in the 2013 regular season, the third-most among quarterbacks. — *JOE BARRENTINE/Staff photographer*

Game Date: October 17, 2013
Location: Glendale, Arizona
Score: Seahawks 34, Cardinals 22

DOMINANT DEFENSE LEADS TO VICTORY

Seattle moves to 6-1 for first time in team history

By Todd Dybas

Whipped to the ground over and over, Arizona quarterback Carson Palmer spent most of Week 7 of his 11th season on his rear.

The Seahawks sacked the veteran seven times, crunching him with defensive tackles, ends and linebackers. Eight different players worked on their post-sack celebrations at Palmer's expense Thursday night in Seattle's 34-22 victory.

Linebacker Bruce Irvin chatted him up.

"I said, 'Man, you're going to be sore,'" Irvin said. "He told me he's used to it."

The Seahawks dominating games on defense continued a norm, too.

After a quick start, Seattle pushed ahead 31-13 and held on Thursday night at University of Phoenix Stadium.

The Seahawks moved to 6-1 for the first time in franchise history in a place they had won just once during the past seven tries.

They have already matched last season's total of regular-season road wins with three.

"We're still not playing as clean as we want," coach Pete Carroll said. "We still have not had the across-the-board clean game we're looking for. It feels like we're still growing.

"We have enough firepower in a lot of areas to overcome the things that are going in the wrong direction."

Much of the arsenal remains on the defense.

Cornerback Brandon Browner bounced back a week after being benched and had an interception he returned to the Arizona 1-yard line. Safety Earl Thomas took advantage of yet another tipped pass that Browner broke up for an interception of his own, his fourth of the season.

The Cardinals averaged just 1.7 yards per rush. A 6-foot man falling forward would have been more effective.

"Whole lot of hungry dudes," Irvin said of the defense. "Bunch of crazed dogs, man."

The defense again compensated for an overall game without rhythm.

Russell Wilson fumbled twice when he was sacked from the back. Arizona converted one of his fumbles into a one-play drive when it scored from the 3, cutting the Seahawks' lead to 14-10 just before halftime.

The Seahawks were stuffed on fourth-and-1 from the Arizona 43 early in the second quarter. The Cardinals picked up three points afterward,

After losing to the Cardinals in his NFL debut in 2012, Russell Wilson put them away handily in their first meeting in 2013, passing for 235 yards and three touchdowns. — *AP Images*

though they went only 26 yards on 10 plays.

The Seahawks also had 10 penalties.

"We have enough playmakers on this team that we can overcome all of that," wide receiver Golden Tate said. "Once we eliminate all that? Watch out. We're going to be very, very dangerous."

Wilson was effective through the air, throwing for 235 yards and three touchdowns on 18-for-29 passing.

He also amazed at times. His conversion of a third-and-3 at the Arizona 48 with Arizona linebacker Daryl Washington around his feet and knocking him down was memorable.

"It was a huge play," Arizona coach Bruce Arians said.

Marshawn Lynch ran 21 times for 91 yards and a score.

Wide receivers Sidney Rice and Tate had strong performances. Rice, who has been quiet this season, caught three passes for 50 yards and a touchdown. Tate led the Seahawks with 77 receiving yards. Tight end Zach Miller led the team with five catches.

The Seahawks put the game away in the third quarter when tight end Kellen Davis caught a 1-yard touchdown pass and Lynch ran in from 2 yards out. The Seahawks were up by 18 points when Lynch handed the ball to the referee with 51 seconds remaining in the third quarter.

A dominant first half resulted in a small halftime lead for the Seahawks.

Seattle outgained Arizona 210-69 but led only 17-10. Miller, back from a hamstring injury that caused him to miss two weeks, caught a 15-yard touchdown pass with 13:25 remaining in the second quarter to put the Seahawks up 14-0 and make the game appear to be on its way to an obvious conclusion.

The stuffed fourth down and Wilson's fumble changed things during another week when the Seahawks started beating themselves.

Eventually, they grappled back control of the game in the second half behind the defense.

"It's been going that way for a couple weeks now," Carroll said. "We expect our guys to play like that." ■

Tight end Zach Miller connects with Russell Wilson on a 15-yard touchdown reception in the Seahawks' 34-22 victory over the Cardinals. *— AP Images*

Game Date: October 28, 2013
Location: St. Louis, Missouri
Score: Seahawks 14, Rams 9

NOTHING NEGATIVE ABOUT UGLY WIN

Seattle beats Rams with goal-line stand

By Todd Dybas

Ugly is being redefined by the Seattle Seahawks.

Throw out those known definitions that intimate a negative connotation. Ugly for the Seahawks has become a beautiful thing, worthy of a franchise-best 7-1 start at the midway point of the season.

Seattle had another beautifully ugly evening in St. Louis on Monday during a gasping and wheezing 14-9 win over the Rams.

During a game that had all the elegance of a rusted and abandoned car for the Seahawks, the result was that simple yet ever-important three-letter word: w-i-n.

Seahawks coach Pete Carroll stood postgame again using phrases such as "very fortunate" after another narrow road win, lumping this in with the opener at the Carolina Panthers and the rally in Houston.

Neither of those had the Seahawks a yard from defeat with four seconds remaining, however.

The Rams had five shots from the 6-yard line or closer to score the winning touchdown and could not.

On fourth-and-goal from the 2 with four seconds remaining, St. Louis went to the shotgun and quarterback Kellen Clemens lofted a pass toward receiver Brian Quick.

Quick was well-covered by Brandon Browner, the pass was not close to being complete and the Seahawks sprinted onto the field with their most brutish win of the season.

"They just tried me on a simple corner or fade route," Browner said. "They threw it up and I was able to get my hands on the ball and make the play.

"A win is a win. However they come, we take them."

Penalized often and unable to protect quarterback Russell Wilson, the Seahawks gave the Rams numerous chances for an upset.

Wilson was sacked seven times. The Seahawks committed 10 penalties for 83 yards. Marshawn Lynch was held to 23 yards on eight carries. Wilson completed 55.5 percent of his passes.

"Million problems in protection again," Carroll said.

The Rams started at their own 3-yard line with 5:42 remaining and down 14-9. They put together their most effective drive of the night, briskly moving into scoring territory.

"They could do anything they wanted on that drive," Carroll said.

Though he was sacked seven times, Russell Wilson remained composed in the pocket and steered the Seahawks to a close win over the Rams. — *AP Images*

Almost anything. The final score eluded St. Louis.

The first quarter was an abomination and harbinger for the Seahawks. Seattle was outgained 75 yards to minus-1. It was the first time since December 1992 versus Pittsburgh that the Seahawks finished with negative total yards in the first quarter.

Wilson was sacked twice. Lynch gained 1 yard on two carries.

But two interceptions thrown by the turnover-prone Clemens, playing in place of injured starter Sam Bradford, kept the Seahawks in it. Linebacker Bruce Irvin dropped into coverage, jammed the tight end off the line and intercepted Clemens in the first quarter at the Seahawks' 21.

Richard Sherman snagged a wayward Clemens pass for a second-quarter interception to set up the Seahawks at the St. Louis 26 following a 38-yard runback.

Wilson eventually hit Golden Tate on third-and-

goal from the 2-yard line for a 7-3 Seattle lead.

In the third quarter, he hooked up with Tate again for an 80-yard touchdown to finish the Seahawks' scoring on a night they had just 40 offensive snaps, 135 total yards and possessed the ball for almost 17 minutes fewer than the Rams.

"We just couldn't get going at all on offense," Carroll said.

The offensive line was woeful. Wilson couldn't get loose to run, gaining 16 rushing yards, his second-lowest total of the season.

Consistently pressured off the edges, Wilson braced for sacks with a focus on simply maintaining possession of the ball.

"Those guys were obviously bringing pressure all night," Wilson said. "The quarterback coach (Carl Smith) and I were talking about all week, 'If it's not there, sometimes you just have to surrender.'"

It wasn't there on a night when Wilson had his fewest total yards of the season. Lynch had his fewest carries and yards.

Still, the Seahawks have four road wins this season, one short of the franchise record and one more than last year.

"I never get tired, but today, this was the most physical game I've ever played in," safety Earl Thomas said. "I'm mentally drained and physically drained."

But, somehow, Thomas goes home a winner. ■

Opposite: Golden Tate scores his first of two touchdowns against the Rams for two yards; the second was an 80-yard reception from Russell Wilson. **Above:** Wilson's 80-yard touchdown pass to Tate was good for his longest of the season. — *AP Images*

REGULAR SEASON
Game Date: November 3, 2013
Location: Seattle, Washington
Score: Seahawks 27, Buccaneers 24, OT

COMEBACK HAWKS

Seattle overcomes 21-0 first-half deficit against winless Buccaneers

By Todd Dybas

Calm with measured answers, wide receiver Doug Baldwin explained that the extraordinary has become ordinary for the Seattle Seahawks.

The team's resuscitations from dismal circumstance are occurring so often, they seem to have all the flamboyance of toast to the Seahawks.

"It's kind of normal for us at this point," Baldwin said.

Normal this time was the largest comeback in franchise history. After trailing by 21 points during a first-half skull-thumping, the Seahawks moved to 8-1 with a 27-24 overtime win against the Tampa Bay Buccaneers on Sunday at CenturyLink Field.

Beating the Bucs allowed the Seahawks to sidestep infamy as the first team to lose to the hapless crew from Tampa Bay (0-8) this season.

It also trumped a rally from 20 points behind at Denver in 1995 for the new franchise comeback mark.

It felt like the reawakening against the Houston Texans in Week 4, when the Seahawks returned from a 17-point halftime deficit to win in overtime.

It carried atrocious stretches of play trumped by Russell Wilson's majesty and Seattle's defensive shifts.

Yeah, normal.

"It doesn't matter what adversity we are going to face, whatever the deficit it is, we are going to pull it out," Baldwin said. "I don't think we doubted it one bit. We've been in these types of situations before. Never 21-0 before, but we've been in situations where we've had to crawl back. It's kind of in our nature."

Tampa Bay took a 21-0 first-half lead. Its high score previously this season was 23.

Wilson was intercepted. Lakes High School product Jermaine Kearse fumbled a kick return. Bucs rookie backup running back Mike James ran for 82 yards in the first two quarters, continuing issues the St. Louis Rams highlighted last Monday night as they gouged the Seahawks' run defense.

Tampa Bay converted a staggering seven of eight third-down attempts. Quarterback Mike Glennon had completed 10 of 11 passes at halftime.

The first half turned heads around the NFL. The Seahawks were being bludgeoned at home by the dregs of the league.

"It ain't the outcome we wanted to start out with," cornerback Brandon Browner said.

Kearse scored with 1:40 remaining in the first

Seahawks running back Marshawn Lynch hurdles teammate Michael Robinson for a chunk of his 125 rushing yards.
— *SCOTT STODDARD/Staff photographer*

half as a first step toward change. Former Washington State kicker Rian Lindell's 33-yard field goal on the first drive of the second half capped the Bucs' glory.

"The way it was going before that, who would have believed that?" Seahawks coach Pete Carroll said.

Glennon began to see more pressure. Wilson started to extend more plays. Marshawn Lynch, who carried 21 times for 125 yards six days after getting just eight carries in St. Louis, began to bang away.

Wilson scored on a zone-read quick snap from 10 yards out toward the end of the third quarter.

Then, Golden Tate struck.

Countering common tactics, Tate fielded a punt at his own 4. He accelerated, stiff-armed, cut back

and spun his way to a 71-yard return, setting up the Seahawks at the Bucs' 25-yard line.

Steven Hauschka kicked a 36-yard field goal 13 seconds into the fourth quarter, cutting the Seahawks' deficit to a touchdown.

The resurrection stalled when Wilson was intercepted on a first-and-goal play from the Bucs' 3 with 7:59 remaining.

The Seahawks again chose to use Lynch as a goal-line decoy, running play-action to him. Wilson was intercepted when Tampa Bay safety Keith Tandy leaped to tip the pass then pulled it in.

The stall was temporary. Seattle's defense forced its first three-and-out of the game. Wilson, who took numerous connective tissue-challenging hits, zinged a pass to Baldwin for the tying score with 1:51 remaining.

Tampa Bay gained three yards in the first possession of overtime before eventually punting. The Seahawks ran eight plays, six of which were Lynch runs, to turn the winning field goal into a mere 27-yard attempt.

Hauschka hit.

Only one NFC team has just one loss after the first nine weeks. It's the Seahawks, who have trailed by 17 or more points at halftime twice this season and won both games.

"You've got to rise up to the occasion," Wilson said. "You can't be timid."

It's the new normal. ■

Opposite: Seahawks wide receiver Golden Tate leaves Buccaneers punter Michael Koenen sprawled on the turf during his 71-yard punt return in the third quarter. — *SCOTT STODDARD/Staff photographer*
Above: Buccaneers running back Mike James passes for a touchdown to give Tampa a 21-0 lead, from which Seattle would come back. — *JOE BARRENTINE/Staff photographer*

25
CORNERBACK

RICHARD SHERMAN

Postgame rant painted inaccurate perception

By Dave Boling • January 21, 2014

Richard Sherman is better than that guy you saw raging into the camera moments after the NFC Championship Game.

He doesn't need me coming to his defense. Nor will he be moved by the advice of an old-school traditionalist that, in the long term, athletes generally don't benefit from spewing inflammatory rhetoric over national television.

But first, sideline interviews conducted moments after a rugged game against a sworn rival are generally worthless and, in some cases, unfair.

And Sherman was caught soon after he made a game-saving pass deflection to deny a receiver with whom he has a contentious history.

The public deserves a fuller picture of Sherman, who came off in this case, to many, as a classless boor.

After the critical play, Sherman confronted San Francisco receiver Michael Crabtree, who had just been beaten in the game's climactic moment. That confrontation went about as you might expect.

Sherman then made a choking gesture to the Niners sideline, one he said was aimed at quarterback Colin Kaepernick. It drew an appropriate flag for taunting.

Sherman then denigrated Crabtree during an interview with Erin Andrews, his hostility said to be the residue of some disrespectful encounter with Crabtree last summer.

One of the best players in the National Football League, Sherman is a major contributor to the Seahawks' success and identity.

But I would suspect that his employers, love him as they surely must, are less than thrilled with the way this reflected the franchise image.

Coach Pete Carroll said the day after the game that he'd already offered counsel because "I want him to present himself in his best light — he's an incredible kid."

And Sherman reportedly texted some media outlets with an apology for drawing the attention away from his teammates.

But that will continue to be the case.

The Super Bowl being the nation's biggest sporting event, taking place in the nation's media

Talking the talk and walking the walk: Seahawks cornerback Richard Sherman tips the pass intended for 49ers wide receiver Michael Crabtree, a climactic play that clinched the NFC Championship Game victory for Seattle. — *TONY OVERMAN/Staff photographer*

capital, Sherman's gestures and comments will be a focus of writers and broadcasters for two weeks, and might divert the positive attention others deserve.

I would hope that analysts and critics — who now have plenty of valid ammunition — make an effort to recognize the full dimension of Sherman.

Those who pop in for a quick listen at his podium on media day won't know that Sherman is perhaps the most likable guy on the team ... always happy, joking, dancing, positive, upbeat.

His media bio will show that he was an honors grad at Stanford, so his intelligence won't come as a surprise. But the breadth of his knowledge and awareness is something you can only fathom over time.

He not only quotes philosophers and classic literature, but has a knack for pinpointing pivotal elements in a debate and analyzing tricky situations. And perhaps adding a few dance steps in the process.

I will openly concede that I am prone to cutting him slack because he's so great to deal with.

In fact, I've been tempted to approach him for advice on everyday things. Richard, what are your thoughts on term or whole-life insurance policies? Blinds versus drapes for my living room? Mashed potatoes or yams with Thanksgiving turkey?

So during the last training camp, I sought out the broader subtext to this athlete who was becoming a highly visible — but not fully understood — persona.

His older brother Branton, who helps Sherman run The Richard Sherman Family Foundation and the "Blanket Coverage" charitable program, told of an off-the-field Richard Sherman dedicated to improving lives of needy local kids.

"Our main goal is to help inner-city kids get adequate school clothing, school supplies, computers, iPads and so forth to help level the playing field," Branton Sherman said. "Because learning is the gateway, learning is the key."

Yes, Branton Sherman said, Richard has always been cocky and combative. But that also fuels his dedication to preparation and his drive to succeed. Even away from the team headquarters, Sherman is never without his computer, studying films of opponents, his brother said.

Sherman does nothing part way, and that's how greatness in many fields is achieved.

He knows as well as anybody the cost of playing this game, the physical toll on the body, the drain of preparation, the frustrations and failures. Everybody on that field is playing at some level of exhaustion and pain.

It should lead a player to respect those who play the game they all love, to honor the brotherhood of the game if not the individual.

He said last week that these games are built from "adrenaline and testosterone" ... and that can be a powerful cocktail.

No one has more fun playing football than Sherman. And I doubt that many have greater appreciation for the privilege of being on a team, given his rise after he was chosen as a fifth-round draft pick.

Few players are as fun to watch. At least until the taunting starts.

I know some players believe the best way to vex vanquished opponents is to ignore them, thereby dismissing them as irrelevant.

But everybody's different, and Sherman has a style that works for him. Above all, to thine ownself be true.

But I've heard that he's been influenced by the career and the personality of Muhammad Ali — certainly an athlete whose societal impact reached a global extent.

And so he might be interested in what the mature Ali said about his cruel taunting of Joe Frazier in his youth.

"I said a lot of things in the heat of the moment I shouldn't have said, called him names I shouldn't have called him," Ali said. "I apologize for that. I'm sorry."

Maybe there's a lesson there from a weathered old champ to a brash young football star. ■

Considered one of the game's premier shutdown corners, Richard Sherman celebrates the NFC Championship Game win with the CenturyLink Field faithful. — *LUI KIT WONG/Staff photographer*

REGULAR SEASON
Game Date: November 10, 2013
Location: Atlanta, Georgia
Score: Seahawks 33, Falcons 10

SEAHAWKS, LYNCH PUNISH FALCONS

Seattle runs away from Atlanta with 'complete-game' performance

By Todd Dybas

So tension-free were the last few minutes, Marshawn Lynch stood on the sideline with his shoes off, jersey pulled up and helmet on top of a water cooler.

The damage done while Lynch was sealed into his highlighter green cleats was the main reason he was at peace well before the game was over.

Seattle's most complete win since a Week 2 dismantling of the San Francisco 49ers came in Atlanta on Sunday. Lynch ran for a season-high 145 yards in the 33-10 bludgeoning of the Atlanta Falcons in the Georgia Dome.

"I thought we played a complete football game with great intensity throughout," Seahawks coach Pete Carroll said.

Lynch seemed to shove aside tacklers the way the Seahawks pushed away the inconsistency of the past few weeks.

"We've been frustrated by it," Carroll said. "We have not been pleased with the way the games have gone. We haven't been able to start and finish a game the way we have been capable. I thought today, we did."

That started with football purity. The Seahawks continue to cling to a run-first approach in the wide-open aerial world of the NFL.

The Seahawks ran the ball 42 times. That was their second-most carries this season trailing the 47 against San Francisco in Week 2. Those two weeks also have the highest carry totals for Lynch this season, 28 against the 49ers and 24 Sunday.

Lynch continues to progress with force. Several times, especially early against the Falcons, Lynch turned poor blocking into positive gains. He bullied with stiff-arms and dragged defenders with churning legs.

Sealed behind his black visor, it's impossible to tell if Lynch's eyes light up when he's about to crash into a defender. His teammates' pleasure is visible, however.

"If he's dominating the game, then, we'll just go ahead and let him dominate the game," wide receiver Doug Baldwin said.

Lynch ran for more than 100 yards for the second consecutive week to help the Seahawks to their fifth road victory of the season, tying the franchise record for regular-season road wins set in 2005.

He even received the ball at the goal line against Atlanta, scoring from 3 yards out, sparing

The Falcons could not contain Marshawn Lynch's Beast Mode as the running back pounds away for some of his game-high 145 rushing yards. — *AP Images*

offensive coordinator Darrell Bevell another week of questions about why Lynch didn't get the ball in goal-to-go situations.

The Seahawks finished with 490 yards. Golden Tate had 106 receiving yards, including a spectacular one-handed catch in the back corner of the end zone.

Doug Baldwin had 76 receiving yards on five catches. Jermaine Kearse had 75 yards and a touchdown on three catches, with one coming against his former Washington teammate Desmond Trufant. The two exchanged jerseys postgame.

The Seahawks led, 23-3, by halftime and never trailed. Steven Hauschka hit four field goals in four tries. The defense easily handled the league's worst rushing offense, allowing just 64 ground yards. The Falcons had a mere 226 total yards. Their only touchdown drive of the day was aided by 35 penalty yards — including two personal fouls — on the Seahawks.

"I think this is our best game all around," safety Earl Thomas said. "You want to be a championship team, you've got to dominate, especially when you get up on teams. You can't let them back in the game.

"I think early on in the season, when we played the Colts, we kind of let guys back in the game. We did a great job of keeping them down when we had them."

At 9-1, the Seahawks extended the best start in franchise history. They have the best record in the NFC. And, for one week, leave the field with a panic-free win. ■

Wide receiver Golden Tate, who had a game-high 106 receiving yards, makes a highlight-reel, one-handed grab in front of Falcons cornerback Robert Alford. — *AP Images*

REGULAR SEASON
Game Date: November 17, 2013
Location: Seattle, Washington
Score: Seahawks 41, Vikings 20

RUN STUFFERS

Seattle shuts down Peterson, heads into bye week on high note

By Todd Dybas

There are the grins that children have when opening an anticipated gift and it looks like a prize plucked from their dreams.

Then there's the postgame look Golden Tate had when asked about fellow Seattle wide receiver Percy Harvin.

Tate smiled, paused and kind of peered into the distance.

"I'm excited," Tate said. "We've got some players."

The proof of that was on the field Sunday, when the Seahawks moved to 10-1 for the first time in franchise history with a 41-20 beatdown of the Minnesota Vikings at CenturyLink Field. It was their team-record 13th straight home victory.

Harvin's Seattle debut juiced a team that has begun to squelch any opposing unit the past two weeks and zips into the bye week with the NFL's best record.

Hammering hapless Atlanta on the road last week provided a feeling of progress. Sunday's thwarting of Minnesota gave a shove to notions that the Seahawks are heading toward full form.

It also spurs the question: If Seattle is 10-1 while getting healthy and into a rhythm, what will it look like afterward?

"We're in a good spot right now," safety Earl Thomas said. "We know that. The big thing about that is you have to be consistent. You can't get too high. You have to stay even-keeled.

"You've got to remember what it took to get to this point. I think this week was our best grind week. It's going to keep getting better if we keep our same mind-set."

The Seahawks' move to 10 wins was made easier by their defense surrounding Vikings running back Adrian Peterson.

Peterson ran for 182 yards on 17 carries when Minnesota came to Seattle last year. He had just 65 yards on 21 carries Sunday. Multiple players hit him. Tackles were helped by linebackers. Linebackers hung on when ends and safeties came to close the play.

The Seahawks crept safety Kam Chancellor up to the same level as the linebackers and inside the edge of the tackles. The box was fully stacked, set to challenge only the Vikings' running game and double-dog dare Minnesota to throw.

It couldn't. Starting quarterback Christian Ponder was intercepted twice. Backup Matt Cassel also was intercepted. The Vikings burned

Safety Kam Chancellor (top) was part of a stout unit that helped limit star Vikings running back Adrian Peterson to 65 yards on 21 carries. — *LUI KIT WONG/Staff photographer*

cornerback Richard Sherman once on a double-move for a deep touchdown but otherwise did little on offense.

"We know what kind of player he is," Seahawks defensive end Cliff Avril said of Peterson. "I've been playing against him for six years. He's a patient runner. Once he hits a gap, he sees it and goes. I think we did a good job of just playing sound defense."

For the second consecutive week, Seattle's offense was powerful.

Even before making his first catch — a juggling third-down conversion in the second quarter — Harvin was causing issues.

The Vikings' safeties often looked at and cheated toward Harvin. Doug Baldwin was left to beat one cornerback and did so throughout. He made a splendid 19-yard touchdown catch in the back corner of the end zone just before halftime to put Seattle in front, 24-13.

Marshawn Lynch had a 4-yard rushing touchdown to end the first quarter. He pulled in a back-handed flip from quarterback Russell Wilson for an early fourth-quarter touchdown that vaulted the Seahawks to a 31-13 lead.

Steven Hauschka kicked two more field goals. He has missed once all season.

Tight end Zach Miller led the Seahawks in receptions (four) and yards receiving (69).

Linebackers Bobby Wagner and K.J. Wright shared the team lead with nine tackles.

Avril forced a fumble.

The Vikings came into the game leading the NFL in punt returns. They had zero return yards Sunday.

Playing in place of injured cornerback Brandon Browner, Walter Thurmond had an interception return for a touchdown.

Defensive tackle Clinton McDonald even had a pick.

Coach Pete Carroll had only one gripe.

"We would like to keep playing," Carroll said.

He won't have a choice to do that with the bye week coming up. It's about the only thing slowing down the Seahawks at this point. ■

Quarterback Russell Wilson, who threw for 230 yards, two touchdowns and no interceptions against the Vikings, eludes defensive end Jared Allen.
— *LUI KIT WONG/Staff photographer*

REGULAR SEASON
Game Date: December 2, 2013
Location: Seattle, Washington
Score: Seahawks 34, Saints 7

MONDAY NIGHT BEATDOWN

Seattle shuts down Brees, Saints passing game

By Todd Dybas

Saints quarterback Drew Brees didn't have a white flag in his hand when he took a knee to close the first half, but he might as well have been signaling surrender anyway.

The Seahawks put together a tension-snuffing performance on Monday Night Football by dismantling the New Orleans Saints 34-7 in raucous CenturyLink Field.

The Saints came to Seattle with a 9-2 record, stalking the Seahawks for potential home-field advantage in the playoffs.

They left dominated. The Seahawks took a 17-0 first-quarter lead on their way to stamping out any doubt about the result, even with Brees at the controls for New Orleans.

The Seahawks are 11-1. They have clinched a playoff spot. They danced, howled and paraded around the field as if having a personal party with 68,387 — a CenturyLink Field record.

"We're not like everybody else," safety Earl Thomas said.

That appeared to be the case Monday night.

The Seahawks, to use Thomas' term, made Brees and stud tight end Jimmy Graham look "normal."

Brees was 23-for-38 and gained a season-low 147 yards. Graham had three catches for 42 yards. The Seahawks lived with check-down throws from Brees and batted away any over-the-top shots.

Per usual, the Seahawks defense was not working from an exotic perspective. They were often in base defense, allowing various defenders to counter Graham when he lined up in front of them.

"We wanted to play our defense, and if they go out there, stand up and beat us man-to-man? Then they deserved to win," cornerback Richard Sherman said.

The Saints used an alternate approach in allowing wide receiver Doug Baldwin to make a 52-yard gain and tight end Zach Miller a 60-yard gain.

The large gains for Baldwin and Miller were the anticipated counters to blitz-enthralled Saints defensive coordinator Rob Ryan.

Seahawks quarterback Russell Wilson signaled to Baldwin to change his route because he identified a pending blitz on his large gain. Wilson threw the ball to a spot as the blitz came. Baldwin was right there up the left sideline.

Miller leaked out up the right sideline and

Seahawks cornerback Byron Maxwell runs away from Saints running back Mark Ingram with an apparent fumble during the Seahawks' win over the New Orleans Saints. Referees later ruled the play an incomplete pass.
— *TONY OVERMAN/Staff photographer*

a rolling Wilson lofted a pass to him. No one was in front of Miller as he began to churn down the field. Eventually, the 255-pound tight end was caught from behind, despite throwing a spin move into the mix.

Fullback Michael Robinson even caught a 21-yard pass.

"We wanted to be great against the blitz," Wilson said. "We like the sense of pressure because there is a lot of green grass behind it.

"We were clicking on all cylinders."

Defensive tackle Michael Bennett went 22 yards for the Seahawks' first touchdown. After defensive end Cliff Avril stripped Brees from behind, Bennett was able to run into the end zone to boost Seattle in front 10-0.

Miller caught a 2-yard pass from Wilson with 1:55 to go in the first quarter and put the Seahawks in front 17-0. There would be no comeback.

Baldwin caught a 4-yard touchdown pass in the second quarter.

Second-string fullback Derrick Coleman caught one of the oddest touchdown passes of the season in the third. Tight end Kellen Davis had a Wilson pass clank off his hands then pop into the air about three yards from the goal line.

In a night crossed with purpose and serendipity, Coleman snagged the ball and dove into the end zone.

The Seahawks led 34-7 after Coleman's unlikely touchdown. The Saints had been beaten, the league had been notified again.

"We feel like we don't get as much credit as we should," Baldwin said. "But that fuels our fire." ∎

Seahawks defensive end Cliff Avril strips Drew Brees, leading to a 22-yard touchdown return by defensive lineman Michael Bennett and pushing the Seahawks to an early 10-0 advantage.
— *TONY OVERMAN/Staff photographer*

29 & 31
SAFETIES

EARL THOMAS & KAM CHANCELLOR

'The best safety tandem in the league'

By Dave Boling • January 27, 2014

Earl Thomas and Kam Chancellor hoped to change Seahawks football.

They may end up changing the game.

Have a pair of safeties ever more perfectly reflected their position names? One so free, the other so strong ... as if designed specifically for their purposes.

Thomas roams sideline-to-sideline, a dervish of a free safety. Chancellor, the intimidating strong safety, causes receivers to scan the field pre-snap, in an attempt to avoid the peril wearing the No. 31 jersey.

"The best safety tandem in the league," Hall of Fame and Gold Standard defensive back Ronnie Lott said of Thomas and Chancellor.

Given their combined 22 interceptions and five Pro Bowl honors in just four seasons together, few would debate Lott's assertion of their positional primacy at the moment.

A more relevant question is how long, if they sustain this pace, before the Seahawks tandem is the best ever?

They're certainly off to a quick start, as Thomas is 24 and Chancellor 25. But the precocious pair had this in their sights from the first day.

"Yeah, we always have talked about changing Seattle," Thomas said. "We came in as competitors, young and probably dumb, but at the same time, we understood that we could make a change and it's definitely panned out for us."

Back in the early days of their partnership, they committed to excelling together, from regular early morning film studies all the way to their offseason gym-rat basketball sessions, when they insisted on being on the same team so they could always work to be athletically in sync.

"We have prepared ourselves for this," Chancellor said. "We're never complacent. We want to be great, we want to separate ourselves. That's been part of our mind-set from the start. You don't say that unless you believe it, and if you're dedicated and determined about it, it can happen."

The two speak as they play. Thomas is all burst and flashes, Chancellor more controlled, but with enormous force.

Chancellor described Thomas: "He's here one second and then, poof! He's gone. He's like the Tasmanian Devil, you know, when he starts spinning. That's what Earl's like."

Chancellor's leadership is quieter but no less

Seahawks defensive lineman Brandon Mebane (top) and safety Kam Chancellor tackle Saints running back Mark Ingram for a loss during Seattle's playoff victory. — *TONY OVERMAN/Staff photographer*

valuable. When yet another league suspension for performance-enhancers hit the Hawks last spring, Chancellor was one who stood up and said, in essence, it's time everybody grows up. And when Chancellor speaks, teammates listen.

"He plays with so much passion, he just loves the game of football," quarterback Russell Wilson said. "You really respect that about Kam — he does this the right way."

They didn't become a true duo, though, until Thomas was ready to accept Chancellor, a fifth-round draft pick, into the partnership.

Thomas had been a first-rounder from Texas (14th pick), while Chancellor was a bit of a tweener at Virginia Tech. At 6 feet 3, 232 pounds, he was the size of some linebackers, and some scouting reports ranked him as the 27th safety prospect in the draft — eight places below Wisconsin's Chris Maragos, who is now a backup safety for the Hawks.

Thomas explained the root connection: "I think it all started when I put my pride to the side and said, 'This guy is just as good as me.' So why not open up to him and tell him all of me? Tell him, 'Man, if you see me doing this, please let me know. Please let me know because on game day, I definitely don't want to be in that position to hurt the team.'"

Chancellor had to earn it, playing behind veteran Lawyer Milloy as a rookie, but growing into the job when Milloy retired.

"When you really are humble about the situation, and really let guys into your world, good stuff like that happens," Thomas said of his relationship with Chancellor. "It's a respect factor."

Thomas and Chancellor, as a subset of the noted secondary dubbed the Legion of Boom, dominated particularly in the Seahawks' four games leading up to the Super Bowl. Chancellor totaled 45 tackles, two interceptions and six passes defensed in that time. Thomas, meanwhile, has generated momentum as a candidate for league-wide Defensive Player of the Year.

"Our safety position is one that you could really see the feature players and the different things they bring to our team," defensive coordinator Dan Quinn said. "What Kam Chancellor puts out on tape ... the contact and the hits that he delivers, he's one of the most physical players that we have. That helps our entire team. With Earl Thomas, it's the speed that he brings to our game. He plays at such a fast pace (with such) instincts and knowledge of the game."

While Thomas, with three All-Pro honors, is viewed as the senior partner, Chancellor has recently won the high regard of observers like Lott, who played 15 seasons in the NFL. Lott gave Chancellor the ultimate compliment for a safety in Seattle, by comparing him to Kenny Easley, a five-time Pro Bowl selection for the Hawks in the 1980s.

"(Chancellor) is getting close to being in that community of greatness," Lott said. "And that is hard for me to say that because I have the utmost respect for Kenny Easley."

The Thomas-Chancellor duo, Lott says, is so effective because of their aggressiveness.

"Those two are playing at that level (and) will be playing a role in this game because they attack people," Lott said.

"We silently push each other," Chancellor said. "When you see your best friend practicing so hard, then, shoot, you've got to step it up, too. Yeah, we're partners, but we're competitors, too."

And neither is satisfied.

"There's plays we've left out there," Chancellor said. "You can strive for perfection, and nobody reaches that, but the striving for it is what can make you great." ■

Ballhawking safety Earl Thomas celebrates the season-ending victory against the Rams to clinch home-field advantage for the Seahawks. — *TONY OVERMAN/Staff photographer*

REGULAR SEASON

Game Date: December 8, 2013
Location: San Francisco, California
Score: 49ers 19, Seahawks 17

HEAVYWEIGHT MATCH

Rival 49ers hand Seahawks their second loss during defensive slugfest

By Todd Dybas

The rancor that filtered through the Seattle Seahawks' locker room after their loss to the Indianapolis Colts in Week 5 was not present Sunday.

Seattle was dealing with its second loss of the season after a late burst by running back Frank Gore put San Francisco in field-goal position, prefacing a 22-yard layup for Phil Dawson that sealed a 19-17 win for the 49ers on Sunday at decrepit Candlestick Park.

General disappointment in losing replaced the bitterness that was present in Indianapolis. The Seahawks are 11-2, still hold a two-game lead in the NFC West and finished Sunday with the conference's best record.

"We're not worried about anything," cornerback Richard Sherman said. "There's no chance for us to be worried about anything. We would have loved to get the win, but it doesn't really change anything for us."

The loss was the Seahawks' first in more than two months. San Francisco snapped Seattle's seven-game winning streak by beating them the heavy-handed way both sides favor.

The Seahawks' Steven Hauschka had squeezed through a 31-yard field goal for a 17-16 lead with

6:20 remaining before Gore's 51-yard run, his longest of the season, yanked the game back into San Francisco's palms.

Gore had 54 yards total before cutting back and zipping through the right side. There was no backside help or safety to be seen, and by the time Gore fell purposely to the ground, the Seahawks were caught in a game dictated by the clock.

"Obviously, somebody messed up," Sherman said.

A quarterback sweep by Colin Kaepernick on a third-and-7 from the Seattle 15-yard line after the Seahawks used their final two timeouts packaged the win for San Francisco. Dawson's kick with 26 seconds remaining closed the box.

A heave from Russell Wilson on the Seahawks' final possession was intercepted at the San Francisco 20-yard line when Jermaine Kearse fell down.

That enabled the 49ers to take a knee and exhale.

"We had them, then we let them off the leash; we had them, then we let them off again," safety Earl Thomas said. "When you're on the road, you have to bring your special teams and defense, and we had mistakes in both of those. It cost us today."

San Francisco trickled out to a 6-0 lead during

Cornerback Byron Maxwell leaps to make an interception in front of 49ers wide receiver Michael Crabtree, who was repeatedly thwarted by the Seahawks during the regular season and postseason. — *AP Images*

a stagnant first quarter for the Seahawks. Seattle gained just 36 yards in the quarter.

Marshawn Lynch's 11-yard second-quarter touchdown run wiped out that lead. Dawson would hit from 52 yards, then Seahawks rookie tight end Luke Willson caught a 39-yard touchdown pass for his first career score, putting the Seahawks up 14-9.

Vernon Davis' 8-yard touchdown reception dragged San Francisco back in front, 16-14, six seconds before halftime.

The expected share of kidney punches and foot stomps from each side was underway. San Francisco and Seattle both strive to play with unmatched force, something they took turns doing Sunday.

San Francisco linebacker NaVorro Bowman spent the game sharing train wrecks with Lynch. Seattle's Chris Clemons hoisted, then planted Kaepernick for a sack. Amid the on-field bell-ringing, a fog horn bellowed whenever San Francisco scored in this antiquated Bay-side stadium.

Even the stiff grass field had a menacing feel, as if beset by rigor mortis. The team will abandon Candlestick next season.

There was no scoring in the third quarter, leaving the fourth to be dotted with the two field goals — one the Seahawks hoped would win, and the other the winner for the 49ers. It seemed like the natural conclusion for two defenses bent on dictating the game.

Pushed during the weeklong run-up were story lines about animosity between the teams. That was not on display after the game in conduct or commentary. Dozens of players shook hands on the field, then players in both locker rooms spoke respectfully about the other.

There was universal agreement about the difficulty of disposing of the other side.

"It feels like you go to the dentist chair and three and a half hours of getting root canal work done," San Francisco coach Jim Harbaugh said of playing the Seahawks. "They're tough. These games are only for the tough." ■

Running back Marshawn Lynch scores on an 11-yard run to give the Seahawks a 7-6 lead in the second quarter. — *AP Images*

Game Date: December 15, 2013
Location: East Rutherford, New Jersey
Score: Seahawks 23, Giants 0

SUPER BOWL PREVIEW

Seattle D picks apart Giants at home of Super Bowl XLVIII

By Todd Dybas

Curled up without a womb to protect him, New York Giants quarterback Eli Manning pulled his knees toward his chest on the MetLife Stadium FieldTurf three plays into his team's first possession.

Manning likely would have preferred to stay there for the rest of the cool and crisp afternoon, but he had to get up and deal with the Seahawks' defense the rest of the way.

It did not go well.

The Seahawks intercepted Manning five times during a 23-0 asphyxiation of the New York Giants at the site of this season's Super Bowl. Seattle moved to 12-2 and is one win from claiming the NFC West and home-field advantage throughout the playoffs. The Seahawks also finished a franchise-best 6-2 on the road this season.

"A complete game," Seahawks coach Pete Carroll said. "All day long, all phases. Sacking the quarterbacks and the picks, it was as complete a game as we've had."

It was Seattle's first shutout of the year and the first time New York went scoreless at home during the regular season since the Dallas Cowboys beat them, 35-0, on Sept. 4, 1995.

So dominant were the Seahawks, the Giants didn't cross midfield until a Kam Chancellor personal foul vaulted them over the brickwalled 50-yard line with 7:35 remaining in the game.

"I think this was one of our best games disguise-wise, communication-wise," said Seahawks safety Earl Thomas, who had an interception. "I think our (defensive) line did a great job of keeping pressure in (Manning's) face, making him step up and scramble for his life. He was just throwing it up.

"We have great guys back there just waiting for games like this, and we capitalized when we had our opportunities."

Out of the litany of evidence that Manning was atrocious and the Seahawks ferocious was this: Seattle cornerbacks Richard Sherman and Byron Maxwell combined to catch more Manning passes (four) than the Giants' top two receivers, Victor Cruz and Hakeem Nicks (three total).

"A pathetic performance," Giants coach Tom Coughlin said.

Part of a defensive effort that forced five interceptions and limited the Giants to 156 passing yards, cornerback Richard Sherman steps in front of Giants wide receiver Hakeem Nicks. — *AP Images*

New York finished with 54 yards in the first half. On its opening drive in the second half, it reduced that total to 44 yards after the series earned minus-10 yards.

While New Yorkers dispersed, the Seahawks took a look around. During the week leading up to the game, Seattle tried to trump two narratives. First, that it would have a hard time getting going after losing to San Francisco, something that proved not to be true.

Second, that it wasn't thinking about the Super Bowl being played at the same site as Sunday's game. That might have been true during the week, but not on Sunday.

"I'd be lying if I said I never thought about it," linebacker Bobby Wagner said. "We know that we have two more games in the regular season and we've got to take care of business in the playoffs to get back out here. If we play our cards right, we'll be back out here."

After not running once last week, Seahawks quarterback Russell Wilson scrambled eight times for a game-high 50 yards. Wilson was 18-for-27 on the day for 206 yards and a touchdown. The offense wasn't spectacular but did enough.

Kicker Steven Hauschka made three field goals — from 49, 44 and 24 yards — and is now 27-for-28 on the season.

The Seahawks gave up 4 punt-return yards. This is news because it's the first time since Oct. 28, a span of five games, Seattle has allowed an inch to a punt returner.

"I really loved the way we played across the board," Carroll said. ∎

Quarterback Russell Wilson, who rushed for 50 yards in addition to his 206 passing yards, stiff-arms Giants cornerback Terrell Thomas. — *AP Images*

Game Date: December 22, 2013
Location: Seattle, Washington
Score: Cardinals 17, Seahawks 10

OFFENSIVE OUTPUT

Arizona snaps Seattle's 14-game home winning streak

By Todd Dybas

Off came his helmet, on went the blue and green winter hat with the pom-pom on top.

Russell Wilson plunked down next to offensive coordinator Darrell Bevell on the white, heated bench midway through the third quarter to look at what just happened after another dysfunctional drive.

They didn't find any answers.

The Seahawks offense moved with the efficiency of a one-eyed man who had his legs tied together Sunday. It led to a streak-snapping and division-title-delaying 17-10 loss to the ambitious Arizona Cardinals at CenturyLink Field.

Wilson had his worst day of the season during his first professional home loss, breaking a streak of 14 consecutive wins. His quarterback rating was 49.6, a sliver poorer than the 49.7 he posted in Seattle's unlikely 23-20 overtime win in Houston in Week 4. He completed a season-low 40.7 percent of his passes.

Which puts any partying on hold.

The Seahawks are in the playoffs. But the division title and home-field advantage remain to be acquired.

More likely, Seattle will have to beat the St. Louis Rams at CenturyLink Field next week, just as in 2010, to lock down the division and a more advantageous playoff schedule.

"We should have won this game" Wilson said.

Three times Sunday, the Seahawks started drives in Arizona territory and did not score. In those three drives, Seattle gained four yards.

Following a Malcolm Smith interception that placed the ball at the 4-yard line with 42 seconds remaining in the first half, the Seahawks put up zero points.

Marshawn Lynch ran up the middle on first-and-goal for two yards. He ran right for no gain, stuffed by menacing Arizona linebacker Karlos Dansby. A third-and-1 pass attempt from Wilson had no chance.

The Seahawks committed a penalty before what would surely have been a simple field goal for Steven Hauschka, who came into the game 30-for-31 on the season. His lone miss was blocked. He had made 22 in a row.

His 24-yard attempt just before the half on Sunday hit the left upright. Even the field-goal post was denying the Seahawks.

"It was hard today," coach Pete Carroll said. "I don't know why we had so much coverage on us

Seahawks running back Marshawn Lynch, who had 71 rushing yards during Seattle's lone home loss in 2013, bobbles the football. — *TONY OVERMAN/Staff photographer*

Palmer, who missed some practice during the week because of a sore ankle, rolled right on third down. Defensive tackle Clinton McDonald pursued. Palmer strung the play out enough to throw just out of the reach of linebacker Bobby Wagner and back to tight end Jake Ballard to convert third-and-3 from the Cardinals' 27-yard line.

"All week they had been saying he has a bad ankle," safety Earl Thomas said. "He looked pretty good out there."

The Cardinals pushed to Seattle's 31-yard line. Palmer, faced with another third down, went to Michael Floyd up the left sideline. Cornerback Byron Maxwell tipped the ball when it initially arrived, yet Floyd still was still able to clamp his hands around it for a stadium-silencing 31-yard touchdown.

Arizona converted the two-point conversion to go up 17-10.

The Seahawks' final drive started with 2:13 remaining. It ended seven seconds later.

Wilson's low pass bounced into the air after hitting Doug Baldwin's outstretched arm and the ground, according to Baldwin. Dansby secured it. After discussion and review, the referees upheld the interception call, citing the lack of "indisputable evidence" on the replay that the pass was incomplete.

For the second time in three weeks, the Seahawks' defense was not able to hold a late lead. Average offensive production — the Seahawks came in averaging 27.1 points per game — would have been sufficient Sunday. Instead, the afternoon's slog likely delays playoff answers for another week. ∎

today. For whatever reason, we just couldn't find guys open."

Yet, Seattle's season-low 10 points were enough for a late lead. Tight end Zach Miller sauntered into the back left corner of the end zone to catch a lofted throw from Wilson. The 11-yard touchdown put the Seahawks up 10-9 with 7:26 remaining.

Two weeks ago in San Francisco, the Seahawks went up 17-16 with 6:20 remaining. The 49ers put together an 11-play, 76-yard drive to align a field-goal attempt. They made it, and Seattle lost.

Arizona had 1:06 more than did San Francisco to do its work, but the odds seemed limited. Quarterback Carson Palmer had been intercepted four times, twice by Richard Sherman.

Opposite: Safety Earl Thomas looks on as cornerback Richard Sherman intercepts the ball in front of Cardinals wide receiver Larry Fitzgerald for one of his two takeaways in the loss. **Above:** Cardinals cornerback Jerraud Powers forces Seahawks wide receiver Golden Tate to fumble. — *TONY OVERMAN/Staff photographer*

REGULAR SEASON
Game Date: December 29, 2013
Location: Seattle, Washington
Score: Seahawks 27, Rams 9

SEAHAWKS WIN NFC WEST

Seattle clinches home-field advantage during penalty-laden contest

By Todd Dybas

Sunday was the time for elation.

Wide receiver Golden Tate lay down in the blue paint of a sideline sign that said, "Thank you 12s." Quarterback Russell Wilson clutched the game ball as he looped around the south stands for high-fives with fans.

The white lights of the CenturyLink Field scoreboard showed the reason: Seahawks 27, Rams 9.

The Seahawks (13-3) won the NFC West division for the first time since 2010. They are the NFC's No. 1 seed heading into the playoffs. They receive a first-round bye and home-field advantage for the postseason.

"We know we had a couple shots at it earlier and didn't get that done, so it was frustrating," coach Pete Carroll said. "When it came time to finish, we did it."

The Seahawks' trifecta of triumphs was sealed at the conclusion of a skirmish- and flag-laden afternoon in front of an announced crowd of 68,264.

The teams combined for 19 penalties. The Rams (7-9) were called for 12. At least three times Sunday, referee Jeff Triplette announced offsetting penalties.

He ejected Rams defensive tackle Kendall Langford when Langford accidentally hit an official's hat. Seattle running back Marshawn Lynch had to be restrained by a half-dozen teammates after a late hit out of bounds sent him to the turf.

St. Louis worked to bait the Seahawks at every turn. With mouths, hands to the face and borderline dirty play, the Rams tried to discombobulate Seattle.

"I think that was probably their plan," strong safety Kam Chancellor said. "Just to get us on the penalty end of the board. But we stayed focused."

Seattle countered the extracurricular activities, for the most part, with calm backed by brawn.

The league's top defense began the scoring when linebacker Malcolm Smith intercepted a pass from Rams quarterback Kellen Clemens for a 37-yard first-quarter touchdown.

Steven Hauschka booted two second-quarter field goals, from 28 and 35 yards, as the Seahawks crept to a 13-0 halftime lead.

Lynch reset himself after being hit out of bounds. He scored a 2-yard touchdown two

Defensive lineman Chris Clemons watches as Seahawks linebacker Malcolm Smith punctuates his pick-six interception for the game's first score by leaping into the end zone. — *TONY OVERMAN/Staff photographer*

Rams rookie running back Zac Stacy gained a season-high 134 yards in the first game against Seattle. He had 15 carries for 15 yards Sunday.

Clemens was intercepted twice. For the season, Clemens has been intercepted seven times. Four of those were against the Seahawks.

Yet, Clemens was thankful for one thing after the game. He scrambled during a fourth-quarter drive and saw Chancellor pivot then start toward him. Clemens waved to Chancellor that he was going to slide in an effort, essentially, not to be mangled by one of the league's most ferocious hitters.

"It was kind of a pull-off wave, I guess," Chancellor said.

Clemens thanked Chancellor afterward. The Rams had been beaten. It was simply time to go home with hides intact.

After the moderate on-field celebration, the music thumped in the Seattle locker room. Players tugged on rigid NFC West Champions hats, danced with varying abilities and looked forward.

The bye week will be used to heal and plan. The Seahawks will host a divisional playoff game in two weeks for the first time since they went to the Super Bowl after the 2005 season.

"I don't think it hit me yet," free safety Earl Thomas said. "I'm just ready for what's coming next. You've got to keep tunnel vision. This is a great stepping-stone. We did what we want. But we've still got some business left out there." ■

plays — and three flags — later for a 20-3 lead with 2 minutes, 21 seconds remaining in the third quarter.

He didn't celebrate much, opting to sternly walk off the field after a group hug. He made his way to the ensuing special teams huddle where he encouraged Chancellor to go do some damage.

Tate's 47-yard touchdown catch in the fourth quarter pushed the Seahawks up, 27-3.

The 27 points were more than sufficient. The Rams scored a late touchdown against a mix of defensive backups.

Before that, there was no movement against the Seahawks' defense.

Opposite: Seahawks running back Marshawn Lynch, who had 97 rushing yards and a touchdown during the victory, breaks away from Rams linebacker Alec Ogletree. **Above:** Known as a players' coach, Seahawks head coach Pete Carroll counsels Lynch during a timeout in the last game of the regular season.
— *TONY OVERMAN/Staff photographer*

GENERAL MANAGER

JOHN SCHNEIDER

He didn't play a down, but Seahawks GM deserved game ball

By Dave Boling • January 23, 2014

The Seattle Seahawks had dramatically subdued the invading San Francisco 49ers, 23-17, and collected in the locker room for coach Pete Carroll's postgame congratulations and praise.

Carroll pointed to the extraordinary efforts of a handful of players that allowed the Seahawks to outscore the Niners, 20-7, in the second half of the NFC Championship Game, earning the team its second trip to the Super Bowl.

But beyond all that, Carroll was so filled with gratitude for the contributions of a specific Seahawk that he made a gesture he normally avoids: He presented a "game ball."

He called up a man from the back of the gathering, one who is practiced at the art of inconspicuousness. Committed to that low profile, the man probably is the only Seahawk to be quoted less than running back Marshawn Lynch.

John Schneider.

If you're relying only on newspaper references or broadcast interviews, you probably wouldn't know that Schneider, the Seahawks' stealth general manager, is the only person whose contributions to this team's success rival or match those of Carroll — his collaborator in rebuilding this franchise.

"I don't give out game balls, because I just don't," Carroll said to the team after the win over the Niners. "But there's one guy I want to point out, the guy who partnered with me every step of the way ... John Schneider is awesome."

The players screamed that Schneider step forward and make a speech.

Carroll gave him a big hug, and in a perfect example of how their relationship works, he then busted on Schneider because his shirt was "pitted out."

At this point, Schneider was springing leaks from his eyes, too.

"I'm so proud of you guys, proud of everybody in this whole room, whole building," Schneider said. "To watch you guys work every single day.... I've watched a lot of you guys since you were, shoot, freshmen in college, even. Every one of you is so special. I'm just really proud of all you guys ... let's go kick some ass."

There are a couple of clues in that statement

John Schneider, a protégé of legendary Packers general manager Ron Wolf, watches the Seahawks team, which he built, during a training camp practice. — *JOE BARRENTINE/Staff photographer*

that help us understand Schneider. Yes, he does watch the team practice every day, and a number of players have told me they respect that in a man who makes life-altering personnel decisions.

And, yes, he's such a dogged evaluator of talent that he sometimes starts zeroing in on prospects before other GMs might know they exist.

And if there's a message he wanted to send to these men — almost all of whom are there because of his efforts — it's that he very sincerely expected them to go kick some ass Feb. 2 in Super Bowl XLVIII.

When Carroll was given the power to pick the GM, and he and chief executive officer Tod Leiweke arrived at the 38-year-old Schneider, it seemed likely that he was positioned to be Carroll's lieutenant rather than full managerial partner.

But at one point during that news conference, Schneider came up with an answer that hinted that there was so much more depth and grit to him, that he had the chops to be his own man.

He was asked about his time in the Green Bay Packers' front office, and which of their successful drafts or acquisitions were the result of his scouting.

Schneider declined to answer. No, he stressed, that's not how it works. And with that single answer, he showed an attribute rare and crucial to success — the absence of ego.

A couple of weeks earlier, when Carroll was asked about his relationship with Schneider, he talked about their communication and shared vision. "I think it's absolutely the most crucial relationship," Carroll said.

They melted down the transaction wires the first year or so and are now so deep they can withstand injuries and suspensions without losing a stride.

And they rebuilt it so quickly and so thoroughly, they go to the Super Bowl in their fourth year with a team that started the season with the fourth-youngest roster in the NFL.

Look at the NFC Championship Game win: Undrafted find Doug Baldwin led the team in receiving. Lynch (picked up cheaply from Buffalo) led the team in rushing. Fifth-rounder Kam Chancellor had an interception, and the game-saving pick was tipped by All-Pro cornerback Richard Sherman (fifth-rounder) to seventh-round linebacker Malcolm Smith.

Another key turnover was a fumble caused by Cliff Avril and recovered by Michael Bennett, two key free-agent acquisitions before the 2013 season.

Schneider and the Hawks have had some draft and free-agent whiffs, but those happen, and the bull's-eyes have been so spectacular, they more than compensate.

The most compelling of those is the discovery of quarterback Russell Wilson in the third round. A two-time Pro Bowl selection, Wilson is the franchise cornerstone for the future. Hawk fans should enjoy the rewards of Wilson's talents for years.

Think back to the aftermath of the Seahawks' last Super Bowl appearance, after the 2005 season, when the flawed relationship between coach Mike Holmgren and GM Tim Ruskell helped cause the team to start coming undone.

Schneider and Carroll proved this is a collaboration that not only works, but appears sustainable. ■

Egoless Seahawks general manager John Schneider fist bumps wide receiver Golden Tate during practice. — *JOE BARRENTINE/Staff photographer*

NFC DIVISIONAL PLAYOFFS
Game Date: January 11, 2014
Location: Seattle, Washington
Score: Seahawks 23, Saints 15

SEAHAWKS POUND, GROUND SAINTS

Lynch's running carries offense to divisional-round win

By Todd Dybas

Gold-embossed headphones were clamped onto Marshawn Lynch's head after the game during another succinct conversation with the media.

Gold chains hung on top of his broad chest. He answered quickly, then left, delivering another full day of what Lynch has come to be known for: ferocious action and few public words.

Lynch ran for a Seahawks postseason-record 140 yards, once again starring as the central figure in a 23-15 grind-house divisional-round playoff win over the New Orleans Saints on Saturday in a dank and wind-whipped CenturyLink Field.

The Seahawks advanced to the NFC title game for the first time since the 2005-06 season, when they made the Super Bowl for the only time in franchise history.

Lynch's coffin-sealing 31-yard touchdown run with 2 minutes, 40 seconds remaining in the fourth quarter was the conclusion of a day based in battering.

The Seahawks ran 35 times and threw just 18, choosing not to tango with a brisk wind from the south and instead feed Lynch.

His 28 carries tied a season-high. The 140 yards were 5 fewer than his season best at Atlanta.

Just more than three years after he scored an iconic 67-yard touchdown against the Saints which resulted in the earth shaking, Lynch did in the Saints again.

"I don't know if it's the opponent or just when we play the Saints, we run the ball," fullback Michael Robinson said. "We wanted to beat them up a little bit. It's playoff time. We want to test your chin a little bit."

Lynch exemplified that with his usual forceful runs. The capper was his 31-yard touchdown around the left side to put the Seahawks in front 23-8. Once he made the corner, Lynch had a clear line to the end zone. He slowed temporarily to add a stiff-arm to the run.

There were times — though rare — during the day when Lynch was banged backward. However, thinking of those runs had Robinson shadow boxing at his locker.

"Body blows, body blows," Robinson said. "The 1, 2 yards. The zero yards. Those are body blows. The 1s and 2s will eventually get going."

Most of the day was a slog for the Seattle offense. Russell Wilson was not crisp, misfiring slants and finishing 9-for-18 passing.

Seahawks running back Marshawn Lynch drags Saints cornerback Corey White into the end zone during his 15-yard score in the second quarter. — *TONY OVERMAN/Staff photographer*

"Just on me," Wilson said. "That's something I can fix. I'm not worried about it."

The Saints at times gambled with cover-zero blitzes. Wilson burned them in the regular-season meeting Dec. 2 when they blitzed multiple players, leaving wide receivers with one-on-one coverage.

Wilson sniffed out the Saints' intent on third-and-3 from the Seattle 45-yard line with 2 minutes, 57 seconds remaining in the game. He changed the protection, then lofted a pass up the left sideline for Doug Baldwin.

Baldwin was able to turn back, snag the ball with two hands and get a knee down before he went out of bounds. The 24-yard reception was the Seahawks' longest and most important catch of the day.

Lynch scored on the next play, and any push back from the Saints seemed stifled.

"He just continues to crank it out for us," Seahawks coach Pete Carroll said.

With 2:40 remaining, the Seahawks led 23-8. Just more than two minutes later, the lead was 23-15 after a 9-yard touchdown pass to Marques Colston.

New Orleans lined up for an onside kick, which bounced to Seattle's Golden Tate, who slid to the ground and tried to smother the ball. It clanged off his chest, allowing Colston to recover at the Saints' 41-yard line.

The Saints were out of timeouts. Brees hit Pro Bowl tight end Jimmy Graham, whom the Seahawks silenced throughout the day, for an 8-yard gain. It was Graham's first catch and came with 24 seconds left in the game.

Brees spiked the ball to stop the clock. His next pass was complete to Colston, then, inexplicably, Colston threw a forward pass to the opposite side of the field. The Saints appeared to be attempting a form of a throwback, last-ditch play. But Colston's botched pass resulted in an automatic 10-second runoff of the clock and ended the game.

"We'll look at the film, next question," Saints coach Sean Payton said when asked about the play.

Lynch scored a 15-yard touchdown in the first quarter to push the Seahawks in front 13-0. Two first-quarter Steven Hauschka field goals had put the Seahawks up, 6-0. Hauschka was 3-for-3 on the day. He joined Lynch in being able to succeed though the rain and the wind.

Lynch hadn't run for more than 100 yards since Nov. 10, though he was just short when he finished the regular-season finale against St. Louis with 97 yards.

But his Saturday rumbling left the Seahawks 60 minutes from a second Super Bowl appearance.

"Whoever is coming here, just be ready to play because we damn sure will be," Seattle defensive lineman Red Bryant said. ∎

Opposite: Marshawn Lynch breaks free from the New Orleans defense for a chunk of his game-high 140 rushing yards. **Above:** Despite being soaking wet, Seahawks head coach Pete Carroll has reason to smile during his team's decisive 23-15 victory over the Saints. — *TONY OVERMAN/Staff photographer*

NFC CHAMPIONSHIP GAME

Game Date: January 19, 2014
Location: Seattle, Washington
Score: Seahawks 23, 49ers 17

BACK ON THE BIG STAGE

Seattle advances to Super Bowl with game-saving interception vs. 49ers

By Todd Dybas

Standing in a dark tunnel at MetLife Stadium in mid-December, Seattle Seahawks fullback Michael Robinson told his teammates to look around.

Robinson wanted them to understand the field, the slopes, what it feels like in the locker room. He wanted them to store that information for one reason.

"We're coming back here," Robinson said.

An end-zone tip from Richard Sherman turned Robinson into a soothsayer Sunday. Sherman's coverage, coupled with 10 unanswered fourth-quarter points, produced a 23-17 Seattle win over the Seahawks' mightiest rival, the San Francisco 49ers, in the NFC Championship Game.

The Seahawks lived to play the Denver Broncos in Super Bowl XLVIII at MetLife Stadium in East Rutherford, N.J.

The organization's second trip to the Super Bowl was more anticipated than the first in 2006. Since summer, the Seahawks were swarmed with expectations. As the NFC's top seed, they had the luxury of playing in the noisiest homestead in the NFL. There could be no better scenario for such an indomitable home team.

Sunday's win washed away any lingering memories of last season's last-minute defeat to Atlanta in the playoffs. Sherman's tip in the end zone of a fade pass from San Francisco quarterback Colin Kaepernick was caught by linebacker Malcolm Smith with 22 seconds remaining. In a blink, the 49ers were out of leverage and, three plays later, forced to exit.

Sherman had been thrown at once prior in the game. That Kaepernick, who was intercepted twice, tested him again in the most crucial time, allowed the in-your-face Sherman to be at his all-time brashest afterward.

"When you try the best corner in the game with a mediocre receiver, that's what happens," Sherman said. "Game."

Robinson left the field with tears coming down his face, saying afterward he thought his career was over in the exhibition season when he became sick and was cut.

"Today was just our day," Robinson said. "Losing was not an option. It was not on the table. It was not a choice."

Red Bryant, a native of Jasper, Texas, explained

In a matchup between two young quarterbacks, Seattle's Russell Wilson had the better performance, giving him the opportunity to hold up the championship hardware. — *LUI KIT WONG/Staff photographer*

Wilson from the pocket and leading to a fumble Smith recovered.

It was a stunning start. Off the first-snap play-action, Wilson had tight end Zach Miller open downfield. Instead, the 49ers took over at the Seahawks' 15-yard line 10 seconds into the game.

But the Seahawks defense held San Francisco to a 25-yard field goal.

The 49ers led before those that filled the stadium even wrapped their heads around the fact the game had started.

That lead grew to 10-0 when backup running back Anthony Dixon sprung over the top of the Seahawks' defensive line on 4th-and-goal from the 1-yard line. It was set up by Kaepernick torturing the Seahawks with his running.

The Seahawks' offense sputtered throughout the first half. Wilson was erratic. Marshawn Lynch was often stuffed. San Francisco linebacker NaVorro Bowman patrolled the middle of the field like an unfed pitbull on watch at the junkyard.

how he would watch the Dallas Cowboys dynasty when he was younger and dream of the Super Bowl. It was a repeated thought throughout one of the NFL's youngest locker rooms. When quarterback Russell Wilson was squeezing the last seconds off the clock with each kneel-down, dreams of being in a place most never go and many envision were coming true.

"It hit me with 22 seconds to go," left tackle Russell Okung said. "We're here."

The arrival was in doubt much of the game. The ferocious 49ers immediately reminded Wilson of their linebackers' speed. Aldon Smith tracked down Wilson on the game's first play from scrimmage, flushing

Finally, a break. Doug Baldwin leaked behind the San Francisco defense and caught a 51-yard pass. The drive only netted three points on Steven Hauschka's 32-yard field goal. San Francisco led 10-3 at the half.

Lynch broke through in the third quarter with a 40-yard touchdown run around the left side. After so many brutish collisions in the middle of the line with angry 49ers defenders, Lynch finally found outside space when he bounced off backup lineman Alvin Bailey. Bailey's use in the Seahawks' jumbo package as the extra blocker changed the course of the running game.

The fourth quarter was a game unto itself. Flags plopped to the ground signalling to the Seahawks a free

Opposite: Seahawks cornerback Richard Sherman deflects a pass intended for Michael Crabtree in the Seattle end zone late in the fourth quarter. **Above:** Sherman has words with Crabtree following the play, which sealed the victory for Seattle. — *TONY OVERMAN/Staff photographer*

play was under way on fourth-and-7 from the 49ers' 35-yard line after San Francisco jumped offside. Each receiver went deep, Wilson took his shot and Jermaine Kearse clamped the ball to his body on a game-changing touchdown.

The catch vaulted the Seahawks into a 20-17 lead. Mania followed.

Kearse fumbled when hit over the middle near the goal line. The loose ball landed on Bowman, who mangled his left leg on the play, and fell to the ground with the ball. Once the pile was cleared, Lynch held the ball. By rule, the play could not be reviewed and became a gift for Seattle.

In a striking reversal of fortune, Lynch fumbled the next play. San Francisco recovered, but Kaepernick started to crumble.

Kaepernick committed three turnovers in the fourth quarter. First, he was stripped from behind by Cliff Avril. Then, Kam Chancellor intercepted him on the sideline, which led to the final score of the day, a 47-yard field goal from Hauschka. Sherman's tipped ball for a pick was the final door slam.

"We needed to take the next step," Seahawks coach Pete Carroll said. "Finish this football game playing better than they did longer, and our guys got that done."

Green and blue confetti sat on the field afterward. Hours after the screaming had ceased, and Frank Sinatra's "New York, New York" had been turned off, only television camera lights dotting the sideline remained. The home of the NFC champions was silent after its most extreme opponent had been vanquished in front of a record crowd.

"It doesn't get any better," Wilson said. ∎

Wide receiver Jermaine Kearse comes down in the end zone with a touchdown reception to give the Seahawks a 20-17 lead early in the fourth quarter.
— *TONY OVERMAN/Staff photographer*

127

While nesting in the heart of the 12th man, Seahawks mascot Blitz cheers during Seattle's playoff victory over New Orleans. — *TONY OVERMAN/Staff photographer*